Studies in
Writing & Rhetoric

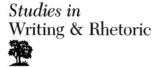

IN 1980, THE CONFERENCE ON COLLEGE COMPOSITION AND COM-
munication perceived a need for providing publishing opportunities
for monographs that were too lengthy for publication in its journal
and too short for the typical publication of scholarly books by The
National Council of Teachers of English. A series called Studies in
Writing and Rhetoric was conceived, and a Publication Committee
established.

Monographs to be considered for publication may be speculative,
theoretical, historical, or analytical studies; research reports; or
other works contributing to a better understanding of writing, including interdisciplinary studies or studies in disciplines related to
composing. The SWR series will exclude textbooks, unrevised dis-
sertations, book-length manuscripts, course syllabi, lesson plans,
and collections of previously published material.

Any teacher-writer interested in submitting a work for publication in this series should send either a prospectus and sample manuscript or a full manuscript to the NCTE Coordinator of Professional
Publications, 1111 Kenyon Road, Urbana, IL 61801. Accompanied
by sample manuscript, a prospectus should contain a rationale, a
definition of readership within the CCCC constituency, comparison
with related publications, an annotated table of contents, an esti-
mate of length in double-spaced 8½ × 11 sheets, and the date by
which full manuscript can be expected. Manuscripts should be in
the range of 100 to 170 typed manuscript pages.

The works that have been published in this series serve as models
for future SWR monographs.

Coordinator of Professional Publications, NCTE

Toward a Grammar of Passages

Richard M. Coe

CONTRIBUTING RESEARCHERS: SUSAN FAHEY,
SUN-I CHEN, ZHU WEI-FANG, JIA SHAN,
WENDY WATSON, CAMERON MARTIN,
AND NING YI-ZHONG

WITH A FOREWORD BY GWEN BREWER

Published for the Conference on College
Composition and Communication

SOUTHERN ILLINOIS UNIVERSITY PRESS
Carbondale and Edwardsville

Production of works in this series has been partly funded by the
Conference on College Composition and Communication of the National
Council of Teachers of English

Printed in the United States of America
Designed by Design for Publishing, Inc., Bob Nance
Production supervised by Natalia Nadraga

Library of Congress Cataloging-in-Publication Data

Coe, Richard M.
    Toward a grammar of passages.

    (Studies in writing & rhetoric)
    "Published for the Conference on College
Composition and Communication."
    Bibliography: p.
    Includes index.
    1. English language—Rhetoric—Study and teaching.
2. English language—Grammar—Study and teaching
(Higher) I. Conference on College Composition and
Communication (U.S.) II. Title. III. Series.
PE1404.C57 1988   808'.042'07   87-9894
ISBN 0-8093-1420-7

91 90 89 88   4 3 2 1

To
Paule and Sasha,
who gifted me much happiness
during the years I nurtured this text,
and to
Ellen, who gifted me the seed

Contents

FOREWORD by Gwen W. Brewer   ix

PREFACE   xi

1. The Task   1

2. Theory, Purposes, and Contexts   5
    Defining the Problem   5
        Reading and Writing   5
        Cohesion Cues and Semantic Structure   7
        Inductive and Deductive Paragraphs   9
        Ambiguity and Objectivity   10
    The Christensen Tradition   12
    Confusions and Conflations   18
        Invention and Arrangement / Form and Process   19
        Abstraction and Generality   22

3. The Discourse Matrix   26
    Key Concepts   26
        The Unit of Analysis   27
        Three Basic Relationships   27
        Subordination   29
        Coordination   30
        Superordination   31
        Specific Rhetorical Relations   32
        Stadia, Idea Strings, and Node Strings   33
    Techniques   34
        Ambiguities   37

232399

4. Applications 42
    Standard Structures 43
        When Is a Paragraph? 44
        Specialized Discourses 48
        Pedagogy 49
    Contrastive Rhetoric 53
    Poor Writing 61
    Pedagogy 65
        Thinking 65
        Writing 67
        Reading 69

5. Implications 73

APPENDIXES
A. Generalization and Abstraction 79
    Richard Coe, Wendy Watson, and Susan Fahey
B. Other Instruments 83
    The Nold and Davis Matrix 83
    Topical Structure Analysis 86
C. Further Hypotheses 90
    Paragraphing 90
    Punctuation 91
D. Practice Passage 95

NOTES 97

GLOSSARY 107

WORKS CITED 111

AUTHOR INDEX 121

Foreword

Gwen W. Brewer

MINA SHAUGHNESSY OBSERVED THAT WHAT BASIC WRITERS LACK is a certain kind of language. Good writers, in contrast, possess a fluency that allows them to produce "a flow of sentences" from an internalized "grammar of passages." With this analogy, Shaughnessy suggests a metaphorical relationship between the sentence and longer passages. We are all familiar with the grammar that generates and analyzes sentences, but we lack an efficient system for generating, analyzing, and evaluating paragraphs and longer passages.

Richard M. Coe and his associates have evolved such a "grammar" of passages, one useful for both research and pedagogy. It consists of a matrix analysis which, by means of a relatively simple graphic instrument, connects meaning to structure and clarifies the relationships of the sentences in a passage.

This matrix analysis evolved out of two sources: Francis Christensen's generative rhetoric and Ellen Nold and Brent Davis' graphic representation of semantic relationships. Christensen's generative rhetoric of the sentence and of the paragraph set up a means of generating and analyzing the levels of generality and the patterns of modification in a passage. Though useful and influential, this analysis is cumbersome because it requires the rewriting of all the sentences.

Nold and Davis set up a three-dimensional graphic matrix which used lines and numbered circles to analyze paragraphs. They used their matrix to illustrate sequential rather than logical relationships among sentences. The complexity of the matrix precluded its being widely used.

Coe has created a functional instrument for textual analysis of passages by modifying and integrating these two systems. He simplified the Nold and Davis instrument into a two-dimensional graphic matrix consisting of numbered circles and connecting lines. This matrix he superimposed on the Christensen rhetoric that analyzes logical semantic relationships among sentences so effectively. Coe's instrument gives us a visual picture of the coordinate, subordinate, and superordinate relationships among sentences in a passage.

Coe's matrix analysis will be useful to the researcher, the teacher, and the writer. Through analyzing the structure of a paragraph or longer passage, it can help identify the characteristics of a rhetorical community, delineating the contrasting rhetoric of languages or disciplines. Coe's colleagues, for example, have identified a traditional rhetorical pattern in Chinese: a recurring spiraling structure that presents a pedagogical problem because it is not recognizable in current English rhetoric. Chinese students, therefore, have had difficulty writing in the expected English structure.

The matrix has a broad and flexible range of applications. It could be used to enable contrast of characteristic patterns in scientific as opposed to general exposition. In the literary field, it could be used to identify stylistic characteristics common to twentieth-century women novelists. In teaching, it could be used to identify strong or weak elements in student writing, or be used as an empirical tool to help the students teach themselves how to write and punctuate effectively. In reading, the matrix could help students derive the meaning of a passage by helping them to identify contextual clues and to understand the relationships among main, subordinate, and superordinate ideas.

Researchers, teachers, and writers will find Coe's formulation useful. Through it, many students will become better writers and readers. In following through on the ideas of Mina Shaughnessy, Coe gives us a solid means of studying and teaching the structure of written passages.

Preface

WHEN SHE LEFT OUR PROFESSION, ELLEN NOLD BEQUEATHED ME an instrument called *the discourse matrix*. I valued it immediately because it proved useful in the particular work that then engaged me: teaching Chinese English teachers at the Shanghai Foreign Language Institute. I valued it ultimately because it promised to shed insight on the aspect of rhetoric which has always been my central interest and concern: *dispositio*, arrangement, organization, structure, form.

In retrospect, I realize that my primary intellectual concern has long been what I now call the rhetoric of form: the relation between form and function, the creative process through which heuristic form guides the generation and comprehension of substance, the formal tyranny of standard structures that constrain against assertions which do not easily fit the form or that motivate us to make statements which readily fit those forms. Even in my undergraduate term papers I see this focus; certainly my master's thesis was what I would now call a case study in the rhetoric of form (specifically, an argument that in *Tiny Alice* Edward Albee invented a new form, parabolic realism, *because* the standard forms of absurdist drama would not carry his meaning effectively).

Many questions about the nature and functions of form cannot be well answered without better instruments for fuller and more precise description of forms. This book, the specific result of Ellen Nold's gift, proffers one such instrument.

A Note on Authorship

We are increasingly aware of writing—especially invention—as a social process. Our theory and research confirm that the stereotype of author as radical individual, suffering in the garret while producing works of genius, deflects our attention from important aspects of the writing process. It deflects our attention, for instance, from the influence of discourse communities on the creative process, from the various senses in which writing is always collaborative (cf. LeFevre and works cited therein).

We understand that the conventions of authorship—and the expectations of readers—often demand some degree of falsification. We know, for example, that certain popular novels are written by teams of researchers, writers, and editors; but only, say, James Michener's name goes on the cover. This is not entirely unfair: Michener is the primary author, and we do not have an adequate formal convention for crediting secondary authors.

Although in traditional terms I am the author of this book, it is in fact very much a collaborative invention. With the exception of a very few paragraphs, I did all the "actual writing" (that is to say, the drafting, the articulation, the putting into words and putting into order). The central "inspiration," the core concepts that focus the theorizing and research, were also "mine" (except insofar as I have taken them from previously published work, which is accordingly cited). But if revision is really part of the "actual writing" process, the concepts you will read are not entirely "mine." They began as such, but were revised collaboratively whenever they proved inadequate to particular tasks. And the research presented to support and develop those revised concepts, although guided by me, was done by others, mostly graduate students. Although in traditional terms I wrote the book and in real terms I am its primary author, to count me as its only author would give the lie to our fine and important theories about writing as a social and collaborative process.

Yet to list as authors all those who made significant contributions to research and revision would also be inaccurate and unfair. Various individuals deserve credit for their contributions to the development and verification of particular concepts. They have also contributed useful secondary research (e.g., on Chinese grammar and rhetoric). But they do not deserve, or want, responsibility for the whole. They do not *authorize* this text.

According to the traditional conventions of authorship, this book can be represented only as authored individually or authored jointly. To represent it as authored individually violates what we are coming to understand about writing as a social and collaborative process. It also underestimates the contributions of those I would call "contributing" authors, who by convention could be credited only in acknowledgments and notes. But to represent it as authored jointly also distorts the actual collaborative process and overestimates those contributions.

In an attempt to be true to the actual process, and as a step toward creating a convention more in keeping with current theory, the title page indicates this book was written *by* me *with* a number of contributing researchers. Wendy Watson, Susan Fahey, and Sun-I Chen made significant contributions to theory and context (chapter 2); Chen, Fahey, and Cameron Martin to method (chapter 3); Fahey, Chen, Zhu Wei-fang, Jia Shan, and Ning Yi-zhong to empirical research (chapter 4). These contributions go beyond what could be fairly credited in acknowledgments and notes, but Watson, Fahey, Chen, Zhu, Jia, Martin, and Ning should not be held responsible for errors in parts of the text to which they did not contribute. For better and for worse, that primary responsibility is mine.

Ac-Knowledge-ments

I am pleased to acknowledge Ann Berthoff, Karen LeFevre, and Stephen Witte, who made useful criticisms of the draft, thus helping me avoid errors and faulty explanations. Knowledge being what it is, I should also ac-knowledge several formative communities without which I would not have produced this book.

The basic conception of form, which has informed virtually all my work in rhetoric and composition theory, was shaped among a community of graduate students in and around the Literature Department at the University of California, San Diego. A proof of this can be seen in a very different book, Don Wayne's *Penshurst: The Semiotics of Place and the Poetics of History*, which applies a similar conception of form to cultural criticism. Even for those of us who never took seminars with them, that community was informed by several young professors, especially Anthony Wilden and Frederick Jamison, and the texts they led us to. Without the conception of form and forming I acquired in that community, I probably would not have formulated my questions about rhetorical form in the ways that led to this study.

I should acknowledge, too, a community of composition faculty at Central Michigan University, who initiated me into the discourse community to which this book is addressed, and thus gave me the terms and traditions in which I have articulated both the central problem and this attempt at its partial solution. On the side, we also created what in the early 1970s was probably the most advanced composition/rhetoric program in North America. Dave Hay, Dave Higgins, Regina Hoover, Bob Kline, and Dean Memering contributed most centrally to my initiation. It was the juxtaposition of this discourse community's traditions and practices with concepts and methods from the UCSD community that allowed me to develop the particular insights which the Conference on College Composition and Communication has decided to publish in the series Studies in Writing and Rhetoric. And that decision to publish is but the last of a series of kindnesses I have experienced from the larger community represented by CCCC, especially from senior members who welcomed and encouraged me when I was still a rather clumsy novice. Edward Corbett, Richard Larson, Erika Lindemann, and Gary Tate were particularly gentle and helpful.

More recently, a smaller community in the Fulbright Program at the Shanghai Foreign Language Institute, 1981–82, saw value in the particular instrument I am presenting here as one step toward a solution to one part of the larger problematique. This community included some eighty-five Chinese teachers of English, several administrators, and my two Fulbright colleagues, Irene Brosnahan and Ann Johns, with whom I taught that year in a closely collaborative, warmly wonderful program. Had they not seen value in the early work, I probably would not have continued.

I take responsibility for this text; if the whole be judged of little use, I take the blame for wasting readers' time. But if the whole (or the tenor) is socially useful, that is because I have created as a member of these communities. I thank them for making this labor more than individual, thus less than alienated.

A Note on Notes

Notes are a problem these days, with many readers and editors expressing a "strong preference" that writers should avoid notes even in scholarly texts. I suspect three interrelated reasons for this fashion. First, the presence of many notes is taken as a signifier of a text that will be difficult to read. Second, for most readers a superscript numeral indicating a note interrupts the flow of the text, as they look down to the bottom of the page or flip to the end of the chapter or text—and usually find some secondary information they do not really want or need, at least not at that moment. Third, publishers increasingly make the interruption worse by opting for endnotes rather than footnotes, primarily because footnotes cost more at the compositor's.

Those readers who hate footnotes—a significant faction—will no doubt be relieved to learn that some hundred notes in the original draft have been reduced to about thirty. Having surrendered to current fashion, however, I feel I must also demur.

In practice, avoiding notes usually means moving into the text proper material that traditionally would have been in footnotes. The other alternative is to delete, choosing clarity and readability over precision and fullness. But the purposes of academic writing are at times reasons for preferring precision over readability (where the two genuinely conflict). Though academese can all too frequently be improved by deleting gobbledygook, rigorous precision and fullness do sometimes demand that academic discourse take the longer way round. Thus discursive footnotes are a device for uncluttering the main text: a discursive footnote provides extra detail or digression for those readers who may want it in a place where other readers can readily ignore it.

Unfortunately, many readers do not find notes easy to ignore— not so many, perhaps, as feel compelled to answer the telephone whensoever it may ring, but still a significant number. In deference to them, I have reduced the number of notes. Let me assure them, moreover, that while they may miss something useful or interesting, they will miss nothing essential if they ignore all notes and appendixes.

Toward a
Grammar of Passages

1

The Task

The mature writer is recognized not so much by the quality of his individual sentences as by his ability to relate sentences in such a way as to create a flow of sentences, a pattern of thought that is produced, one suspects, according to the principles of yet another kind of grammar—a grammar, let us say, of passages.

—Mina Shaughnessy (226)

THE CREATION OF A "GRAMMAR OF PASSAGES" IS ONE OF THE URgent tasks facing composition theorists and researchers, rhetoricians, and teachers of writing. Various goals in these areas cannot be achieved without such a "grammar."

Except to those who already have an intuitive grasp of the underlying cognitive structures, the vocabulary with which we traditionally discuss the structure of passages—e.g., "topic sentence and support"—is woefully inadequate to describe the actual structure of modern English prose, let alone writing from other cultures or historical periods. For one thing, that vocabulary names only two levels of generality, whereas a typical modern English explanatory or persuasive paragraph, it will be suggested below, contains three or four. To understand the ways in which various structures are persuasive in particular contexts, to understand the creative and communicative functions of structure, and certainly to help writing students learn new structures efficiently, we need a better "grammar of passages."

Crucially important questions about the creative and communicative, cognitive and social processes of writing take us beyond the limits of the sentence. To answer these questions, we must understand relationships among sentences within texts as well as relationships between texts and various contexts. But how much can we say about the relationship between language and thought without describing the semantic structure of discourse? What can we say about the function of forms in the creative process without describing the structure of form in the text? What can we say about the interpenetration of cognitive and social processes without defining the socially conventional structures individual writers learn from their cultures and use in their writing? Even to ask such questions rigorously—let alone to answer them in ways useful to writers and teachers of writing—we must be able to describe the structure of texts more fully and precisely than we now can. Both as rhetoricians, who seek to understand the ways in which language is suasive, and as teachers who seek to help writers create (which is to say, help them form, help them create cosmos out of chaos—or re-form, create a better cosmos), we need a "grammar of passages."

Since the renaissance of scholarly interest in composition during the 1960s, the main focus has been on the composing process; and until the mid-1970s, the specific focus was on discovery, the first department of classical rhetoric (Latin *inventio*; Greek *heuresis*). There has also been substantial work on sentence structure; combined with earlier work in stylistics, this has given us considerable theory and research in the third department of classical rhetoric, style. Despite some significant work on paragraphing and cohesion, however, we have not paid comparable attention to the department of classical rhetoric concerned with the literal composing (i.e, "putting together"), with the selection and arrangement of "arguments" into meaningful and effective patterns (Latin *dispositio*; Greek *taxis*). Style was the strongest department of traditional composition theory and the pedagogy of invention has been developed over the past two decades, but arrangement has been neglected, at least until very recently.

Mina Shaughnessy's phrase "a grammar of passages" is a metaphor for a kind of text analysis focused on that quality in texts which is analogous to syntax in sentences. The metaphor has a certain power and clarity which justifies its use: we do need an instrument that will do for groups of sentences what grammar does for an individual sentence—that is, explain how the constituent parts compose the whole and thus which patterns are preferred, which proscribed.

Like any metaphor, however, Shaughnessy's can be misleading if taken literally: overrating the analogy between the structure of sentences and the structure of passages is the fallacy that generated many of the false ideas we now teach about the Paragraph. Though it will analyze the structure of passages much as sentence grammar analyzes syntax and will enable generative-transformational acts, the sort of text grammar we need for dealing with reading and writing will not be literally a grammar.

The simplest, most promising, most elegant attempt to approach the "grammar of passages" is represented by a series of articles and chapters published over the past two decades, largely in *College Composition and Communication*, beginning with Francis Christensen's work in the mid-1960s. I dub this *the Christensen tradition*, defining the central assumption thusly: that classifying statements according to relative level of generality and analyzing patterns of modification among the items so classified is a key to the "grammar of passages." This notion, from Christensen's "A Generative Rhetoric of the Paragraph," is our starting point.[1]

More recently, Ellen Nold and Brent Davis developed a discourse matrix, an instrument for diagramming the relationships defined by the Christensen tradition. Although Nold and Davis' matrix was perhaps the most promising attempt at a "grammar of passages" to date, it contains unresolved contradictions and its three-dimensional complexity makes it impractical for pedagogical applications, unwieldy even for research.

A more practical two-dimensional matrix will be presented here. The basic concept underlying this new matrix remains approximately that first articulated by Christensen and first presented graphically by Nold and Davis. This revised matrix is simple enough for classroom applications and yet capable of representing even more complexity than is the Nold and Davis matrix. To demonstrate the power of this new instrument, I will discuss empirical studies in which it has been used, present further hypotheses generated with its aid, and suggest pedagogical applications.

Relatively brief experience with the new matrix indicates its potential to yield significant insights in various areas and also to serve various pedagogical purposes. It has produced suggestive insights into the structure of passages and into the basis upon which writers paragraph. It can be used to describe the structure of passages within specialized discourses, such as various types of "technical" writing. It has been used to describe structural differences in discourse between cultures and promises similar insights about differences across disciplinary boundaries. It can help explain precisely what is "bad" about the structure of passages that do not work. It can be used by teachers to help students understand particular structures that are being taught and also directly by students or other writers to investigate either their own writing or a type of writing they wish to learn. It may even help explain certain punctuation decisions, particularly the use of such punctuation marks as the colon, semicolon, and dash. Framed by concepts from the New Rhetoric and the Christensen tradition, the matrix may also contribute to unifying disparate aspects of composition theory. Properly contextualized, the matrix can help articulate crucial questions about the relationships between form and function, cognitive and social processes, language, thought, and culture.

The primary purpose here is not to present the sometimes fascinatingly suggestive results of the particular studies (which were done with varying degrees of rigor indicated by their individual contexts); rather, I am using these studies to illustrate the power and potential of the discourse matrix and the concept it represents. I will argue that this sort of description has tremendous power both as a research instrument and as a pedagogical instrument, that it can help us understand the distinct rhetorical structures of different cultures, subcultures, disciplines, and even tasks within particular communicative contexts, and—equally important—can help students understand what we want them to do in particular communicative contexts. Indeed, it was this last need—specifically, to help Chinese teachers describe for Chinese students the mandatory and preferred structures of English professional discourses—that triggered the work presented here.

2

Theory,
Purposes, and Contexts

And the nature of the human mind itself, with the function of abstraction rooted in the nature of language, also provides us with "levels of generalization" (to employ Korzybski's term) by which situations greatly different in their particularities may be felt to belong in the same class (to have a common substance or essence).

—Kenneth Burke (*Philosophy* 3)

. . . [T]he topics of invention, the patterns of arrangement, and the stylistic aspects of sentences, when they reveal similar conceptual structures, are . . . symbolic manifestations of the same underlying thought patterns.

—Frank D'Angelo (*Conceptual Theory* 28–29)

Defining the Problem

Reading and Writing

Readers' abilities to recognize—even (or perhaps especially) subliminally—formal patterns of development allow them to "process" text (i.e., to understand it) efficiently. Writers' abilities to use formal patterns particular readers will recognize allow them to communicate accurately and effectively.

Walter Kintsch argues that comprehension requires knowledge which functions as a frame, helping readers structure information presented by a text. As an example, he cites a paragraph, the first sentence of which refers to a war, thus activating the "War" frame. His "War" frame includes slots for (1) actor, (2) opponent, (3) cause, and (4) outcome ("On Modeling Comprehension" 180–84).[2] Extending Kintsch's argument, I posit a comparable function for formal rhetorical frames: in addition to conjuring the necessary contextual knowledge (e.g., about war), good readers note that a particular passage is an introduction, a definition, or whatever—and read it accordingly.

To perceive or to create coherence, not to mention sense, one must mentally represent the gist of the semantic structure of the text. To plan or substantively revise a piece of writing, one must consider that representation, matching the structure of the plan or draft to the evolving gist. It is significant in this regard that the revising processes of novice writers typically do not involve revising goals or main ideas. Bereiter and Scardamalia hypothesize that novice writers cannot revise "at high levels because they have not constructed the mental representations they need for reprocessing at these levels." Finding that novice student writers could neither summarize the semantic hierarchy of the texts they themselves wrote nor state the gist of experimental texts they were asked to revise, Stephen Witte hypothesized that perhaps they could not distinguish

> between "content" which could be deleted and not alter the gist of the text and "content" which when deleted would alter the gist. . . . Perhaps unskilled writers tend to revise primarily at the word or sentence level because they have never learned how to . . . respond to overall semantic structure of texts, or to evaluate semantic structure against their intentions. ("Topical Structure & Revision" 334–35; cf. Perl, Sommers, and Flower et al.)

By helping composition teachers to analyze and describe formal patterns more precisely and explicitly, a "grammar of passages" would enable them to teach their students how to perceive structure—hence how to create and revise structure. Composition is, at center, a forming process, but what Richard Larson wrote a decade ago has only just started to change in the past five years: "The array of critical and pedagogical pieces on [form and structure] to date highlights problems and uncertainties, but provides few insights" ("Structure and Form" 71; cf. D'Angelo, "Modes of Discourse"). And even these recent studies have concentrated mainly on cohesion, topic sentences, and paragraphing.

We do not yet have a clear enough understanding of the process by which writers' purposes are transformed into foci and thence into textual structure. Nor, although there has been some theorizing in this area,[3] do we have a detailed understanding of how available structures influence the substance of texts. We have traditionally considered "content" as an aspect of invention, the first department of classical rhetoric, while treating structure separately as an aspect of arrangement, the second department. Mixing logical categories, we put something called "drafting" in between invention and revision; and under this heading we discuss such functions as finding focus, selecting from and arranging what has been invented—as well as developing and articulating substance that might be only implicit in the invented material. The process by which we find form, create structure, is the crux of composing, and also the part of the process we have most difficulty directing with precision. An improved ability to discuss the structure of texts is one step toward a better understanding of the process by which we create that structure—as well as of the functional relation of that structure with communicative contexts.

Goetz and Armbruster argue that research on arrangement has been blocked by researchers' methodological biases. It is difficult, they assert, to explore "text structure" independent of "content," to explain "connected discourse" without considering meaning. But the domination of empirical research by behaviorism has denigrated as "mentalistic" and unobjective research techniques dependent upon the determination of meaning (201–2; for a discussion of these concepts in relation to composition theory and research, see Berthoff, "Is Teaching Still Possible?" esp. 743–48).

Cohesion Cues and Semantic Structure

The problem is the relationship between language and meaning. The text can be analyzed as an object, i.e., "objectively," but meaning is in no sense an object. Meaning is a *relation* constructed by readers between text and contexts. Research guided by the "implicit assumption that text structure and content are inherent *in* the text" fails "to come to grips with the constructive, interactive nature of comprehension" (Goetz and Armbruster 202, emphasis added). Research on reading and discourse comprehension demonstrates that "meaning and coherence are not inscribed in the text, . . . but arise from readers' efforts to construct meaning and to integrate the details in the text into a coherent whole" (Bamberg 419–20), a process which is, by traditional definition, "subjective." Louise Wetherbee Phelps elegantly explains *how* we must understand texts as dynamic (13), grasp coherence as *both* synchronic structure *and* diachronic process (22–23). To understand coherence, she asserts, we must explain the reader's "experience of meaningfulness" that correlates "with successful integration during reading, which the reader projects back onto the text as a quality of wholeness" (21). Indeed, the gist of recent research and theory is that a combination of textual and contextual factors guide readers' construction of coherence. What is ultimately at issue is the relation of the textual pattern to the pattern of meaning, so we must not conflate the pattern of cohesion cues in the text with the pattern of coherence readers construct in their minds in response to the text. As Robin Bell Markels emphasizes, moreover, "a merely semantic definition of cohesion" cannot bring us to an understanding of form ("Cohesion Paradigms" 451). Readers' experience of texts as integrated wholes is contextual, substantive, and formal.

Much recent work has focused not on structure itself but rather on the cohesive devices writers use to signal structure, on the cues which signal the "syntax" of passages. This work on cohesion does not comprise a "grammar of passages." Indeed, without a "grammar of passages" its application is limited because only the correlation between cohesion cues and the structures they signal makes the cues significant. One of the most interesting questions is how skillful writers know which structures should be signaled and when the text will be coherent without such cues (presumably because the "implicit" structure will be apparent to the intended readers). We need, therefore, the ability to describe the structure itself, somewhat independently of the cues writers use to signal structure. This need creates problems, however, because the structure of passages depends on meaning (i.e., on semantics and pragmatics) to a much greater extent than does the grammar of sentences. When the study of cohesion is focused on such devices as transition words, there is a clear distinction between the structure of meaning and the transitions which signal that structure. Once we start looking at cohesion created by the repetition of certain words and phrases that name unifying topics—Alton Becker's "lexical equivalence classes," Witte's "topical structure," Markels' "recurrence chains"—the distinction becomes less clear, and it becomes possible to confuse the cues signaling the structure with structure itself. Such confusion is unfortunate because it blurs what ought to be the key question: What is the relationship between cohesion cues and the structure they are presumed to demarcate?

Witte, for example, has devised an instrument which diagrams rather objectively the relationships among the words and phrases that serve as grammatical subjects of the T-units in a passage.[4] This is, of course, not the same as diagramming the meaningful relationships among the statements asserted by those T-units. Because the grammatical subjects are nouns, pronouns, and noun phrases that name what the T-units are about, because the items being diagrammed *are* (to use Becker's phrase) *lexical cues* to the chain of meaning, the results of topical structure analysis do correlate fairly well with analysis of meaning itself. But it is important to remember that topical structure analysis is analysis of cues which generally correlate with meaning, not of the statements which actually constitute the meaning of a passage (cf. Berthoff, "Is Teaching Still Possible?" 746–47). The distinction between topical structure analysis and matrix analysis can be made clear by applying both instruments to the same piece of writing. (See appendix B after reading chapter 3, below, which explains how discourse matrix analysis works.)

Inductive and Deductive Paragraphs

An extreme version of this confusion between linguistic structure (cohesion) and thought structure (coherence) is found in those textbooks which misuse the terms *inductive paragraph* and *deductive paragraph*. What most people conjure as a typical English paragraph, as taught by traditional textbooks, begins with a topic sentence but is based on inductive reasoning. Some texts call such paragraphs deductive just because the generalization precedes the inductive proof, but it is grossly misleading to imply that the same reasoning may be inductive or deductive depending not on the structure of the reasoning but simply on the placement of the topic sentence. Contrary to the usage in some textbooks, it is important to reserve the term *inductive paragraph* for any paragraph based on inductive reasoning. If the proof structure of the paragraph is inductive, we should not call that paragraph deductive just because it begins with a topic sentence. For that matter, we might be best off reserving the terms *inductive* and *deductive* for thought processes, leaving the correlation between logical and rhetorical structures to be demonstrated empirically, not presumed terministically.

Ambiguity and Objectivity

A very basic problem arises because the "deep structure" of a passage is tied to the logical relationships among the statements its sentences assert in a way that the deep structure of a sentence is not. Though grammarians can achieve a kind of objectivity by ignoring meaning when they analyze sentence structure, one cannot describe the structural relationships among sentences without considering the meanings of those sentences. Although readers read sentences and consider propositions represented by those sentences, a "grammar of passages" is concerned with a subset of those propositions, the ones readers would take the text to be asserting; by approximate and in a sense paradoxical analogy to what Michel Foucault analyzes on a much grander scale (cf. pages 73, 74–5 below). I call those propositions *statements*.

As Markels points out, even a discussion of cohesion may need to account for "inferred propositions," which are not actually represented in the words of the text ("Cohesion Paradigms" 455). Whatever "grammar of passages" one devises will inevitably represent the structure of readers' interpretations, their recognition and understanding of statements. Thus, despite similarities implied by the metaphor "grammar of passages," a useful "grammar of passages" cannot be independent of meaning as a grammar of the sentence can be. Rather, it will be based on the relationships among the propositions understood to be asserted by the passage—propositions which can be named only by interpreting the text (and which include only some of the propositions a logician would find in the text). There is immense potential for ambiguity in the reading process which transforms sentences on the page into readers' understanding of the text as a structured set of statements. As Gary Sloan emphasizes, "ambiguity of relationship *is* common, almost the norm at times" ("Transitions" 451). Perhaps this is why Shaughnessy calls for "*yet another kind* of grammar" (emphasis added).

If we define ambiguity as William Empson does—"any verbal nuance, however slight, which gives room for alternative reactions to the same piece of language" (1)—we must conclude that the alternative reactions to an ambiguous text can produce several accurate descriptions, which terribly complicates the task of devising a "grammar of passages." As Paul Ricoeur has emphasized, natural languages are polysemic—that is, it is the necessary "property of words in natural language" to have "more than one meaning." "The simplest message conveyed by the means of natural language has to be interpreted because all the words are polysemic and take their actual meaning from the connection with a given context and a given audience against the background of a given situation" (102).[5] Ambiguity, Ricoeur asserts, "appears to be the permanent counterpart of polysemy, the price to pay for a polysemic language" (102). As Burke argues, moreover, ambiguity is often functional, desirable, for unambiguous (monosemic) language is sometimes an oversimplification of real complexities and contradictions: "Accordingly, what we want [when dealing with such topics as human motives] is *not terms that avoid ambiguity*, but *terms that clearly reveal the strategic spots at which ambiguities necessarily arise*" (*Grammar* xviii).

Ambiguity is thus a necessary and desirable feature of human discourse, which a "grammar of passages" must accommodate, not avoid. For a "grammar of passages," unless it confines itself to surface features, such as cohesion cues, which can be "objectively" catalogued, is ultimately a "grammar" of the cognitive structure represented by the passage. However unsatisfying it may be to those accustomed to the "objective" precision of grammatical analysis, this sort of discourse analysis is *by the nature of the case* the best that can be done without sacrificing the purpose of doing the analysis in the first place. The problem is a cluster of interrelated complexities:

1. We need to describe the structure of passages, not just the cohesion devices which signal that structure.

2. Perhaps because not enough research effort has focused on rhetorical arrangement, we do not yet have the necessary instruments to describe the structure of passages precisely.

3. Any such instrument, because it must analyze meaning, inevitably describes readers' comprehension of texts, not texts isolated from readers.

4. Researchers who hold traditional scientific/empirical values are uncomfortable with the inevitable variations that follow when we describe readers' comprehension of ambiguous texts.

5. But texts are frequently (often necessarily, even desirably), ambiguous and it is the meanings of texts (i.e., reader comprehensions) which concern us.

To some extent, this problem needs to be resolved by researchers and theorists being a bit more sensitive to the particularities of language when they import empirical methods into the discipline we call composition. Beyond that, however, we do need to devise methods that are in some significant sense objective to be used for the close analysis of the structure of passages.

The Christensen Tradition

It is in the Christensen tradition that we find the potential for handling significantly ambiguous passages and also for analyzing the structure of meaning itself, not just cohesion cues which signal that structure. Arguing by analogy from the principles he asserted about sentences in "A Generative Rhetoric of the Sentence," Christensen proposes that subordinate sentences within a paragraph modify the topic sentence in essentially the same way that free modifiers modify the noun and verb heads of a sentence. According to Christensen, the key to understanding the structure of paragraphs lies in the patterns of modification among sentences. And as Michael Grady, Frank D'Angelo, and others have demonstrated, this concept is not limited to paragraphs.

The notion that more general terms or propositions encompass less general terms or propositions can be illustrated by relatively concrete examples:

Detroit, Los Angeles, the United States, Michigan, San Francisco, Canada, California, Ontario, Toronto, Ottawa, North America, Quebec, Montreal, British Columbia, Vancouver, Nova Scotia.

Canada encompasses the provinces of Ontario, Quebec, British Columbia, and Nova Scotia (among others), while Ontario encompasses Toronto and Ottawa. Similarly, the United States encompasses Michigan and California, while California encompasses Los Angeles and San Francisco. And North America encompasses both Canada and the United States, conceptually as well as physically.

A significant pedagogical demonstration of the power of the concept of level of generality can be found in the *Project Literacy Staff Development Manual* chapter on paragraphing (98–125), which I take to reflect the influence of W. Ross Winterowd. This chapter shows how children too young to learn the concept abstractly can be led from their understanding of the relationships among terms like *fruit, apple, banana* to an intuitive understanding of how level-of-generality relationships underlie paragraph structure.

By analogy with the way modifiers work in sentences, Christensen thinks of subordinate T-units as modifying the more general T-unit that semantically encompasses them. The point can be illustrated by the following sentence of William Faulkner's:

Joad's lips stretched tight over his long teeth a moment, and
he licked his lips, like a dog, two licks, one in each
direction from the middle.

"Like a dog" modifies "licked his lips," a relatively general description which could encompass various other types of lip-licking. Similarly, "two licks" starts to explain how a dog licks its lips, hence is more specific than "like a dog." And "one in each direction from the middle" explains "two licks" even more specifically. Christensen represents this analysis schematically by retyping the sentence:

Joad's lips stretched tight over his long teeth a moment,
and he licked his lips,

like a dog,
two licks,
one in each direction from the middle.

Here is a paragraph with comparable structure:

When it was first implemented, the Michigan Terminal System was a
leader in ease of use. But now it has been bypassed.
Other systems now offer features MTS users need.
These features have come to be considered standard.
User friendly, formatted wordprocessing is the most obvious
example.

In "A Generative Rhetoric of the Paragraph," Christensen defines
two relations among levels of generality: subordination and coordination. That is, a given statement may be less general than or on the
same level as the statement preceding it. David Karrfalt asserts that
coordination and subordination are not the only possible relationships; Nold and Davis (141) later credit him with pointing out the
relationship they call *superordination*: a proposition may be *more
general* than the one that precedes it.

The pedagogical significance of Christensen's analyses turns on his
central hypothesis that increased subordination correlates, in general, with quality. As a rule, he argues, readers will get more out
of—and hence evaluate more highly—texts containing denser patterns of modification. This hypothesis is totally consistent with the
practice of most English composition teachers, who regularly encourage students to provide more detail, more examples, more reasons—in general, fuller development. It is consistent with a major
function of writing, especially in schools and other learning contexts, for one advantage of writing (as contrasted with oral discussion or silent thinking) is that the medium tends to encourage fuller
and more precise articulation. It is also consistent with assertions,
like Shaughnessy's, that "the problem in most basic writers' papers
lies in the lack of movement" among levels of generality: their
papers, she affirms, "tend to contain either cases or generalizations,
but not both" (240).

Catharine Keech similarly observes that many papers by basic writers

> seem flawed, not by insufficient concept formation, but by overambitious concepts intuitively derived and inadequately tested. . . . The concepts they were expressing were so broad, that to generate hierarchically organized text they would need to go down the ladder of [generality] to dissect the ideas, analyze them back into their parts, and take the reader back to the original observations to show how they arrived at the concept. (212)

As Eden and Mitchell emphasize, the central virtue of Christensen's model is that it presents writing "as a process of adding, of elaborating on what you have already said." This makes it especially useful "as a diagnostic tool, a guide for writers revising," for it shows writers how to find in what has already been drafted "opportunities for writing more" (422).

Empirical support for Christensen's hypothesis is found in a study by Rebekah Caplan and Keech, the conceptual framework for which was provided by a draft of Nold and Davis' "The Discourse Matrix." Caplan and Keech found a strong correlation between movement through levels of generality and holistic evaluations of student texts. Caplan and Keech's examination of the texts "revealed that the presence of supporting details was an important characteristic" distinguishing papers holistically scored above average from papers holistically scored below average. In an experimental class taught by Caplan, where this concept was emphasized and practiced, students both "increased their use of concrete details," hence the movement through levels of generality, and "improved their mean holistic scores" (109–10).

In "The Ladder of Abstraction," Sarah Freedman and Nold draw the psycholinguistic implication that the pattern of relationships among levels of generality will be "readable" if it matches readers' expectations. Thus we are taken back to Burke's definition of form as "the creation and fulfillment of desire" (*Counter-Statement* 124). The need to relate the rhetorical patterns, which writers use and readers recognize, to cognitive patterns takes us back to Christensen's connection between invention and arrangement. Thus the need to teach students ignorant not only of formal patterns but also of the underlying cognitive processes led Mina Shaughnessy to describe pedagogies appropriate to this aspect of the Christensen tradition (226–56; cf. Shor, esp. chap. 5).

Nold and Davis give us a method for representing relationships among levels of generality that is less cumbersome than Christensen's (which requires recopying the entire passage). They also make several other significant contributions:

1. They relate the Christensen tradition to psycholinguistic theory, especially that of Walter Kintsch.
2. They divide each of the three relationships into three or four types of modification.
3. They assert a relationship between superordination and Paul Rodger's concept of stadia of discourse.

This last gives us a key to a crucial pedagogical question: "When is a paragraph?"

Shortly after Christensen published "A Generative Rhetoric of the Paragraph," Rodgers defined a stadium of discourse as a rhetorical unit "containing a single topic, together with any accrete extensions or adjunctive support." Rodgers argued that these stadia are "the basic rhetorical constituents of prose," which a writer *may* emphasize by setting them off physically as paragraphs. Rodgers thus distinguishes between semantic units on the one hand and the cohesion cue provided by paragraph indentation (essentially a macropunctuation mark) on the other.[6] Briefly, the argument is that the boundaries of stadia and of functional passages (e.g., introductions, transitions exceeding a single sentence) are sites of *potential* paragraph indentation; whether or not writers mark these boundaries depends on contextual variables outside the particular text, such factors as rhetorical context (purpose, audience, and occasion), conventions of "normal" paragraph length in that context, emphasis, and individual proclivities. (Of course, a paragraph indent may also be used just for emphasis in a place where it is not normally an option, just as a dash can be so used within a sentence in a place where there would normally be no punctuation; but such use is, by definition, exceptional.)

Eden and Mitchell dichotomize Christensen, whom they present as epitomizing formalism, and Rodgers, whom they present as "the most important" functionalist (421). There is some truth in their charge that Christensen has formalist tendencies which sometimes, especially when he moves from description to prescription, contradict his own emphasis on a generative rhetoric. And it is certainly true that the type of generation Christensen's approach encourages will occur during revision, which means he will be misunderstood, considered to be contradicting himself, by those who think in terms of "prewriting" and presume generation always precedes revision. As Betty Bamberg suggests, however, coherence is often best generated during revision (426). From this perspective, we can use Christensen and Rodgers together most usefully, for it is the relationship between form and function that we need to explicate.

The type of analysis which comes out of the Christensen tradition can be used for various purposes, and by complementing Christensen with Rodgers, we can emphasize the functional implications of Christensen's formal analyses, thus highlighting what he presumably meant to highlight when he entitled his work "generative rhetoric." On the basis of empirical studies and classroom observations, I will discuss the following potential uses of matrix analysis grounded on the central principles of the Christensen tradition:

1. Matrix analysis can be used as an empirical instrument to verify or challenge standard myths about structure. For example, to what extent is the formula *topic sentence + support* an accurate and adequate description of English paragraphs?
2. Matrix analysis can be used as an instrument for contrastive rhetoric. It can help us describe cross-cultural differences, as well as differences between subcultures, disciplines, genres, and so on. Matrix analysis indicates, for example, that some Chinese and Farsi prose uses structures not commonly found in English. Such findings, if confirmed, would have implications for cross-cultural communication as well as for teaching composition to students whose first language is not English.
3. The matrix can also explain why a passage does not work. It often reveals *what* is "bad" about bad structure.
4. Although this hypothesis is as yet unconfirmed by controlled em-

pirical study, the matrix may explain certain sorts of punctuation. Specifically, it may reveal the structural relationships that cause writers to say two independent clauses are so "closely related" they should be connected by a semicolon (or comma plus coordinating conjunction). Note in this regard Christensen's assertion that punctuation sometimes "should be by the paragraph, not the sentence" ("Paragraph" 155).

5. Matrix analysis can be used by writers who have to write, or teachers who have to teach, a type of writing new to them. For example, a teacher assigned to teach legal prose can use the matrix to analyze the structure of some samples of good legal prose. Such analysis would help the teacher determine what structures are preferred in that discourse.

6. The matrix can be used both in teaching composition and, especially, in teaching composition pedagogy to teachers. In both cases it encourages self-reliance, enabling users to investigate structures empirically for themselves instead of relying dogmatically on assertions they find in textbooks and manuals. Whether or not the matrix itself is explicitly invoked, teachers can use the underlying principles of matrix analysis to help students understand preferred (or required) structures.

7. In a complementary way, the matrix can also be used in teaching reading, for the semantic structures that matter in writing are also basic to reading (e.g., what Kintsch and van Dijk call the "gist" or macrostructure). The matrix both reveals some of these structures and provides a vocabulary for talking about them.

Confusions and Conflations

As is perhaps becoming clear, a number of confusions and conflations in composition theory and terminology prevent us from taking full advantage of the central insights offered by the Christensen tradition. One set of confusions and conflations turns on the interrelation of thought and language, coherence and cohesion, meaning and signification. Related to this set is a certain amount of sloppy usage, including such labels as "inductive" and "deductive" paragraphs. A second set of confusions and conflations, which should be clarified lest what follows be misread, turns on the interrelation of invention and arrangement, form and process. Here, too, a certain amount of questionable terminology complicates the discussion. And third, the basic concept of the Christensen tradition, levels of generality, is itself confused and conflated with several distinct conceptions of generality and abstraction.

Invention and Arrangement / Form and Process

Those who use a process approach with some degree of sophistication regularly recite a litany to the effect that the "stages" of the composing process are discrete, are recursive—are not really stages, just artificial divisions we make for pedagogical reasons. Nonetheless, there is a strong tendency to treat invention (unfortunately often termed "prewriting" as if it were not really part of the "real" writing) and arrangement (organization, structure) as totally discrete. It is questionable to what extent this sharp distinction is an accurate representation of the classical rhetoricians, many of whom seem to have had a much more flexible, dynamic, interactive conception of form as a manifestation of function. At any event, a definitive separation of invention and arrangement implies a conception of form that clearly violates the most basic principles of the New Rhetoric and the implicit axioms of process pedagogy.

In *A Conceptual Theory of Rhetoric*, Frank D'Angelo put the objection this way:

> Following Aristotle's system, I take form to be closely related to the formal principle (i.e., one of the causes of a mode of being) which produces discourse. . . . The formal principle or process of invention is therefore implicit in any discourse. If, for example, the predominant organizational pattern of a mode of discourse takes the form of a comparison, then the writer must have gone through the inventive process of comparing in order to produce that pattern. . . . [P]atterns of development are not only organizational, they are also topical . . . ; that is, they can . . . serve a heuristic function. . . . They are . . . dynamic organizational processes, symbolic manifestations of underlying mental processes, and not merely conventional, static patterns. (56–57)

I. A. Richards made the same point in 1936 when he enjoined us to avoid some traditional mistakes—among them the use of bad analogies which tie us up if we take them too seriously. Some of these are notorious, for example, the opposition between form and content. . . . [Another] makes language a dress which thought puts on. We shall do better to think of a meaning as though it were a plant that has grown—not a can that has been filled or a lump of clay that has been moulded. These are obvious inadequacies; but, as the history of criticism shows, they have not been avoided. . . . (12–13)[7]

Richards' neoromantic assertion that we should think of form as organic (not, in Samuel Johnson's neoclassical metaphor, as a dress that thought puts on) is totally consistent with what was to become one of Christensen's most crucial axioms. For Christensen, form is generative and plastic. The main purpose of his pedagogy is to motivate students to invent new material by showing them how to expand the formal structures they (subliminally) use. Borrowing a concept from Kenneth Burke, I use the term *formal motives* to name the way in which a formal structure motivates writers (and speakers) to invent material. Such titles are important because, so long as we use the old terms, we tend to fall back into the old conceptions[8]—in this case to think of form as a container which we fill with "content," of invention and arrangement as totally discrete departments of rhetoric. When we speak of "form and content," for the most part, we are not even conscious of using a metaphor, so we do not examine the metaphor. We do not ask if, when, and to what extent the relationship between form and subject matter really is comparable to the relationship between a container and something one might pour into it.

In her sweepingly integrative article on the "Dialectics of Coherence," Phelps argues that *process*, as the generative theme of composition studies during the 1970s, tended to create a false dichotomy between process and what was derogatorily termed "product." Except insofar as it arose "naturally" and uniquely from the creative processes of individual writers, form was denigrated as an aspect of "product." Phelps asserts that the process/product dichotomy needs to be transformed into "a dialectic between two processes," writing and reading, with *text* "becoming the third or mediating term." Concepts such as form need to be reconceived as aspects of the overarching process, "the cooperative enterprise whereby writers and readers construct meanings together." This shift, she maintains, "has momentous consequences because it changes the root metaphor of composition from . . . creation to . . . symbolic interaction"

(12–14). One consequence, I believe, is a reconception of form and of its function in the composing process.

Any process approach to written composition, virtually by definition, concerns itself with one or more *how*: how writers create; how writers think, feel, and verbalize to enable writing; how writers learn while writing; how writing communicates with readers; how social processes and contexts influence the shaping and interpreting of texts. Form is dynamically engaged in these processes. Writers create, in part, by juxtaposing inchoate subject matter with rhetorical forms: making the matter fit within the parameters of essay form or memo form or whatever conventional form is used. Similarly, writers think, feel, verbalize, and learn, in part, by using forms of various sorts to discover patterns in the subject. Writing is a social process in large measure because cultural forms, which have been internalized by all properly socialized writers, are used to shape the writing. In many communities those who have not learned the conventional forms are denied access to public media—be that the Gitksan feast hall or the *New York Times* letters column. And reading is certainly enabled by readers' ability to recognize a particular text or part of a text as an instance of a particular form (business letter, extended definition, causal explanation, etc.). Substance *is* the result of processes that synthesize matter and form. "Content" re-formed has been transformed, *substantively* changed—often with the result that meaning has been *significantly* changed. What the neoclassical formalists called "content" is unknowable in its formlessness; it becomes substantive and knowable only when formed.

In this New Rhetorical conception, form is both generative and constraining. Form is empty, an absence; but this emptiness, however plastic, has shape (i.e., form). In human beings, at least, this emptiness creates desire to find what might fill it (or less commonly, to reshape the form to fit the matter at hand). This is part of what Burke means when in "Definition of Man" he wryly defines us as "rotten with perfection" (*Language* 16ff.) In its emptiness, form is heuristic, for it guides a structured search. Faced with the emptiness of a form, a *human* being typically seeks matter to fill it; form becomes, therefore, a motive for generating information—a formal motive.

Except in extreme cases, formal motives interact dialectically with what here may be called *material motives*: having something to say and seeking rhetorical form for saying it effectively. In extreme cases, procrustean forms lead writers, especially less skilled writers, to distort what they had meant to say, or to chose new subject matter which more readily fits the available form. Thus genre—knowledge of genre—becomes a factor in invention. Like any heuristic, form motivates a search for information of a certain type: when searchers can anticipate the shape of stuff they seek, invention is less free but more purposeful; by constraining the search, form focuses attention. Heuristics, in this sense, are distinct from *un*structuring discovery techniques, such as freewriting, which have more to do with *finding* than with using form.

The dominant process pedagogies of the "sixties" pretty much ignored the creative function of form—in part because they were largely concerned with discovery as self-discovery (and thus with the students' experience of discovering form), in part because they were reactions against the static, dogmatic, and inaccurate formalism of prior pedagogies. But forms of various sorts are, in fact, intrinsic to the process of writing. Form and process are not opposites; we need not choose between formalism (the "product" approach) and a process approach to the development of writing abilities. We need, rather, to clarify our understanding of the function of form in writing processes. We need to study form—and forming—much more fully and in many more contexts than we have thus far: form as organic, as structure; as flexible, as rigid; as generative, as constraint—as an instrument of creation and meaning, as the social intruding on the personal. And a "grammar of passages" matters, among other reasons, because a more precise description of particular forms will enable a more profound understanding of how forms function when people write.[9]

Abstraction and Generality

Virtually everyone writing in the Christensen tradition (including Christensen himself) conflates two distinct concepts: level of generality and level of abstraction. Whatever they say, they are really discussing level of generality, but they often confuse this with the "ladder of abstraction" popularized by S. I. Hayakawa (150–66). The failure goes back to the widespread use of the term *abstraction* to describe two distinct cognitive processes, one of which is identical with generalization. To complicate matters, the standard abstract/concrete distinction used by composition teachers to correct their students' style derives from, but is not identical with, the other cognitive process,—that is, from the type of abstraction that is distinct from generalization. In discourse on composition theory and pedagogy, the term *abstract* is used to refer to four distinguishable processes:

1. generalizing (as in inductive reasoning),
2. abstracting as it occurs preconsciously in human perception,
3. abstracting as it functions in concept formation and deductive thinking, and
4. communicating with abstract (rather than concrete) diction.

All four processes are important and relevant to composition, literacy, and education. For our purposes, however, the important point is that only one is generalization. To avoid confusion and conflation, therefore, let us reserve the term *generalization* (or *levels of generality*) for what the discourse matrix represents, leaving the term *abstraction* for the other three related perceptual, intellectual, and linguistic processes.

Generalization is the inductive process by which we reach, say, the concept *bird* by generalizing from robins, sparrows, eagles, geese, ostriches, and so on. Abstraction as a perceptual process allows us to see robins' breasts *as red*, to abstract the redness from the robins (after which we can, of course, go on to generalize about *red things*, including robins' breasts, roses, apples, and perhaps "my true love's lips"). The terms we think of as epitomizing abstraction, such as Love, cannot be reached by simple generalization: though we may generalize from various *loving acts*, we must abstract the "loving" aspect of the concrete act before we generalize. As a conscious intellectual process—and this is another part of what Burke means when he defines us as "rotten with perfection"—abstraction allows us to use abstract ideas in our thinking, as when we use our concept *democracy* to consider the political situation in El Salvador or Nicaragua or our concept *honesty* to decide what to do with a wallet just found. Although derived from this notion of abstract ideas, the stylistic value denoted "Abst" in red ink on the margins of students' papers is rhetorical, referring not to the concept represented by a particular word or phrase but to the effect of that diction on readers

It is true, of course, that generalities tend to be abstract and specifics tend to be concrete (hence the confusion and conflation). But such is not always the case, and the exceptions demonstrate that the concepts are distinct. "Canada" is more general but not more abstract than "Ontario." Statistics, to take a more significant instance, are generally *specific and abstract*; that is why advertising agencies, when they are aiming for emotional impact, will use the example of one hungry child rather than statistics about malnutrition. An infant's cry, unlike a statistic, is extraordinarily concrete but semantically general; it communicates something equivalent to "I want . . ." or "Help me . . ." without specifying what is desired. (Older babies, of course, develop cries that can be interpreted more specifically—though not to the extent believed by parents, who actually rely a great deal on contextual cues.) And a relatively abstract term may also be more specific than a concrete description:

> She felt a stabbing pain in her chest, suffocating difficulty
> catching her breath, dizziness and nausea.

> She had a myocardial infarction.

A doctor who had to prescribe treatment would prefer the second sentence *because it is more specific*. To a nonmedical audience, however, the first sentence seems much more concrete, though it could describe a number of distinct medical conditions. The stylistic concept, abstract/concrete, is about this *seeming*. (For a fuller discussion of the distinction between *general* and *abstract*, see Appendix A.)

Discourse analysis in the Christensen tradition is concerned with *relative* level of generality of propositions or concepts *within a discourse*, as in Christensen's assertion, "There is no theoretical limit to the number of structural layers or levels, each at a lower level of generality, that a speaker may use."[10] It is this notion—levels of generality—that is crucial to analyses of coherence. For a variety of reasons, we must be careful to conflate neither the cognitive processes of abstraction nor the rhetorical *abstract-concrete continuum*, which is stylistic and has to do with the effects of lexical items, with *level of generality*, which has to do with the logic of a piece of discourse (and thus with subordination, coordination, and super-ordination).

Teachers of writing, especially teachers of basic writing, should understand and deal both with levels of generality and with abstraction in its various senses. A complete "grammar of passages" will probably need to take into account the process of abstraction (in Lev Vygotky's sense), but the step toward a "grammar of passages" being attempted here turns on Christensen's concept of levels of generality.

3

The Discourse Matrix

When a supporting sentence is added both writer and reader must see
the *direction of modification* or *direction of movement*. . . . The failure
to see the relation of each upcoming sentence to what has gone before is
probably one source of the difficulty many people have in reading. . . .
The paragraphs our students write are likely to be as thin-textured as
their sentences, and teachers can use this structural analysis of the paragraph to *generate* paragraphs of greater depth.

—Francis Christensen ("Paragraph" 145)

Key Concepts

ALTHOUGH THE ANALYSES DONE IN THE PROCESS OF DEVELOPING
the discourse matrix have suggested modifications of Christensen's
principles, the matrix is essentially a way of representing the relationships among levels of generality/patterns of modification; it is
useful because it allows us to abstract one set of relationships and
represent it schematically, thus emphasizing patterns and allowing
easy comparison/contrasts. It also allows some degree of numerical
and graphic representation, thus facilitating statistical analysis and
allowing some use of computers to do a bit of the drudgery.[11] In
using the matrix, however, it is important to remember that what
really matters is the set of semantic relationships communicated by
the text and reproduced in the matrix drawing.

The Unit of Analysis

Linguistically, texts are composed of sentences. Logically, texts are composed of propositions. For the purpose of discourse analysis, texts are composed of statements, i.e., of the propositions their readers take them to be asserting. Thus a text may contain this sentence:

> Bill watched the red wagon roll toward the barn, but he made no move to stop it.

To a linguist this is one sentence (to a composition specialist two T-units). To a logician, it comprises many propositions (e.g., 'The wagon was red'). For the purposes of discourse analysis, we must decide how many of those propositions to treat as statements. In most communicative contexts, readers will probably take this sentence as making two assertions about what Bill did. For that reason, in doing matrix analyses, we will usually want to take such a sentence as making two statements and ignore all the other propositions.

In practice, to maintain some level of methodological objectivity, we must choose some linguistic unit, usually the T-unit [12] (but sometimes the sentence or the clause), as the unit of analysis. Whatever the unit of analysis, we take the entire unit as a single statement. Though we can move to a smaller unit of analysis, and thus take other propositions into account, at any given level of analysis we usually ignore propositions writers have chosen to subordinate linguistically. In the case of the T-unit, we rationalize this decision by presuming that a writer's decision to put certain propositions in phrases or subordinate clauses is a decision to subordinate those propositions; and though we may occasionally select a proposition the writer has subordinated grammatically, the entire unit is taken as making a single main assertion. Obviously, this involves a pragmatic "rounding off" of the data, a decision to confine the analysis to a particular level of precision. This rounding off is consistent with Christensen's treatment of paragraphs and, though complexities occasionally arise, it generally seems to work.

Three Basic Relationships

The basic principle underlying this type of discourse analysis is that the main proposition represented by a particular T-unit (or sentence or clause) is related to one or more other statements in the discourse in one of three ways: by subordination, coordination, or superordination.

Take, for instance, Paul Rodgers' example from Kipling:

(1) There are nine and sixty ways of constructing tribal lays;
(2) And every single one of them is right!

As the semicolon indicates, the two T-units are coordinate, i.e., two statements on the same level about the same topic (*ways of constructing tribal lays*) ("The Stadium of Discourse" 179). When drawing a matrix, we represent this coordinate relationship with two circles on the same level. (The lines, as will be explained below, indicate logical relationship.)

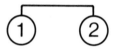

As Rodgers points out, if Kipling's second T-unit had been

(2) Twelve are found in Pakistan, the others in Bombay,

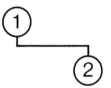

the second T-unit would "merely support the claim made in the first," and "could be removed without disrupting the argument" (179–80). This second T-unit is, in a sense, *encompassed* by the topic (or main proposition) of the first; it is more specific and logically subordinate to the T-unit it inductively "supports." In Christensen's sense, the subordinate T-unit adds to the meaning of the first in the same way that a modifier adds to the term it modifies. To rephrase Christensen's metaphor, a general statement draws a circle within which subordinate statements pirouette.

If on yet another hand, Kipling's second T-unit had been

(2) And lays are only one of many ways to sing a poem.

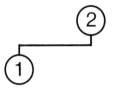

then the second T-unit would encompass the topic of the first; it would be more general than and logically superordinate to the first.

Subordination

A subordinate sentence (or T-unit or clause) can be understood as a kind of modifier, i.e., it modifies or develops the meaning of the statement to which it is subordinate much as an adjective modifies or develops the meaning of a noun. Take, for instance, the following sentences from Strunk and White:

(1) As a rule, single sentences should not be written or printed as paragraphs. (2) An exception may be made for sentences of transition.

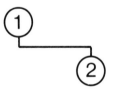

The second sentence is subordinate to the first; it modifies the main proposition of the first in much the same way as the phrase "as a rule" does, i.e., it *qualifies*. Indeed, the second sentence may be considered to develop the phrase "as a rule" by detailing an exception.

Deduction, drawing a specific conclusion from an established generalization, is a somewhat trickier kind of subordination—tricky because people raised in a culture where inductive reasoning predominates tend to see all conclusions as generalizing. Take for example the enthymeme based on a standard syllogism:

(1) All people are mortal.

(2) Therefore, Socrates is mortal.

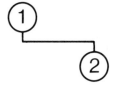

"Therefore" signals a conclusion, but the conclusion is more specific than the proposition upon which it is based. Similarly, the last of the following three sentences draws a deductive conclusion from the preceding two:

(1) Ordinarily writers using description and narration are attempting to create vivid and specific images and ideas in their readers' minds. (2) Cliches ordinarily do not do that. (3) So effective writing generally avoids cliches or uses them in an extraordinary way.

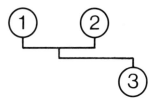

The deduction "modifies" the generalization: logically, it is encompassed by the generalization in much the same way as the concept *red wagon* is encompassed by the concept *wagon* or the concept *rose* is encompassed by the concept *flower.*

In addition to *qualifying* and *deducing,* other subordinate relationships are *defining, exemplifying, giving reasons,* and *explaining* (in the narrow sense of "making plain" by restating more specifically).

Coordination

Coordinate relationships include *repeating,* using other words perhaps, but on the same level of generality, *contradicting, conjoining,* and *contrasting.* Thus the following two T-units from Robert Heilbroner are coordinate, specifically *contrasting:*

(1) Society to Adam Smith was a great family; (2) to Ricardo it was a bitter contest for supremacy.

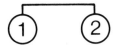

In this next example, adapted from Gary Sloan ("Transitions" 448), the second T-unit is subordinate to the first, and the third T-unit is coordinate *with the first* (specifically, conjoined):

(1) In an earlier age, man was searching for an alternative reality and conceived the unicorn. (2) Alas, that mythic creature is just a horse with a horn. (3) And our imagination continues to be as poverty-stricken as ever in conceiving futures that are alternatives to existing conditions.

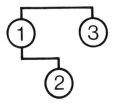

Superordination

Superordination can be divided into three types: *generalizing, commenting,* and *drawing inductive conclusions.* In the second of the following two T-units, Bertrand Russell comments on what he reported in the first:

(1) I do not believe she ever had time to notice that she was growing old. (2) This, I think, is the proper recipe for remaining young.

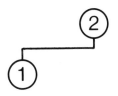

Another version of the same relationship exists in these two sentences that Russell wrote in another context:

(1) Is there objective truth or falsehood in such a statement as 'pleasure is good,' in the same sense as in such a statement as 'snow is white'?
(2) To answer this question, a very long discussion would be necessary.

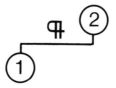

(Note that a writer's decision to paragraph is indicated on the matrix diagram by a paragraph sign, ¶.)

Specific Rhetorical Relations

Especially when resolving ambiguities, it is useful to divide subordinate, coordinate, and superordinate relationships into types. Even if one does not quantify such data, it is useful to know precisely what types of subordination, coordination, and superordination predominate in a particular kind of writing. Though the following categories are tentative, and probably incomplete, they are helpful. Compare Sandra Stotsky's table of semantic categories of lexical cohesion ("Lexical Cohesion" 441).

Coordination:
  contrasting
  contradicting
  conjoining
  repeating (on the same level of generality)

Subordination:
  defining
  exemplifying
  giving reasons
  deducing (i.e., deductive conclusion)
  explaining (i.e., making plain by restating more specifically)
  qualifying

Superordination:
  drawing conclusion, generalizing (inductive inference)
  commenting (on a previously stated proposition)

Note that explaining and generalizing can be similar to repeating—except that an explanation restates more specifically and a generalization more generally. Despite this sense in which restating, explaining, and generalizing are similar, for matrix analysis it is crucial to distinguish them.

Changing (sub)topic, usually to a new aspect of the same general subject, looks like a superordination (at least as diagrammed by Christensen), for it produces a T-unit more general than the one preceding it. The same impression is created on Nold and Davis' matrix, where the relationship is always to the immediately preceding sentence or T-unit. But others, including Karrfalt, believe this contradicts what readers actually do when they read. In fact, changing (sub)topic typically involves a lack of relationship with the immediately preceding T-unit. Psycholinguistically, it is more accurate to see a T-unit that begins a new (sub)topic as readers do, i.e., as subordinate to a previous thesis and/or coordinate to a previous (sub)topic. For the purpose of the analysis is to juxtapose the linguistic *sequence* of the text with the logical *hierarchy* of meaning. On the level of coherence, as Sloan asserts, a T-unit is often "paired not with the one immediately before but with one further removed" ("Transitions" 448), and this is especially true for a T-unit that begins a new (sub)topic.

Stadia, Idea Strings, and Node Strings

Christensen, unfortunately, defines a paragraph as a sequence of "sentences related to one another by coordination and subordination" ("Paragraph" 145). This definition begs the empirical question. We need, rather, to begin by defining paragraphs tautologically as whatever competent writers create when they indent and then to ask what relationships exist within the sequences of sentences competent writers demarcate as paragraphs. We need, therefore, terms other than *paragraph* to entitle sequences of "structurally related sentences."

Rodgers gives us the term *stadium* for a pattern within a discourse sequence which *could* be tagged with a paragraph indentation, i.e., a series of sentences "containing a single topic, together with any accrete extensions or adjunctive support." For Rodgers, a concluding regeneralization at the end of a short passage is part of the stadium it ends—as it should be. This usage is consistent also with the notion of a stadium as encompassing (in the original Greek sense of an oval racecourse) a phase or stage within a process. Because it includes superordination, however, it is not within the letter of Christensen's definition of a paragraph.

Still, Christensen (and later Nold and Davis) are correct in wanting a term to represent a series of T-units uninterrupted by any rise in level of generality, if only so that we can empirically investigate to what extent such strings correlate with the boundaries of what readers perceive as stadia, what writers mark as paragraphs. Let us, therefore, call such a series an *idea string*. An idea string is ordinarily a series of T-units in which every T-unit is either subordinate or coordinate to the immediately preceding T-unit. In practice, it seems easiest to trace idea strings by starting with a specific T-unit and working back to the encompassing generalization.

Idea strings are important structures because they usually represent the simple lineal development of a single statement, which is typically found at the beginning of the string. In practice, an idea string is often identical with a stadium as defined by Rodgers. If a stadium encompasses all the T-units subordinated to a single subtopic, it would ordinarily encompass an idea string; but because it can include, for example, a concluding regeneralization, such as a restatement of a topic sentence, one should say that a stadium tends to begin *before or after* any rise in the level of generality. This distinction is useful and consistent with Rodgers' original definition. The extent to which superordination correlates with stadia boundaries should be determined by empirical investigation, not by overlapping definitions.

Nold and Davis give us the term *node string* for a set of coordinate units, not necessarily consecutive, on the same level of generality. Node strings are important because, within any given topic, the highest node string usually represents the subtopics, the heart of what Kintsch and van Dijk call the macrotext, i.e., the set of gist sentences, the core of what a nineteenth-century English schoolboy might have reproduced as a précis.[13]

Techniques

To do matrix analysis, one first divides the text into units, usually T-units, though the analysis can also be done with larger or smaller units (whole sentences or clauses). These units are then numbered consecutively, and each T-unit is analyzed to determine where it connects to the discourse (usually—but not always—to the immediately preceding T-unit) and whether it is subordinate, coordinate, or superordinate. Although it is not strictly necessary, naming the relationship more specifically, as per the list on page 32, often aids the analysis. To *draw* a matrix, one represents each T-unit by a numbered circle, represents that T-unit's level of generality by the relative placement of the circle on the page, and represents the logical (or "modifying") relationship with a line connecting that numbered circle to another.

The drawing is not essential to the analysis; but it is convenient and efficient. To represent a paragraph from Bergen Evans, Christensen had to reproduce it:

1 He, the native speaker, may, of course, speak a form of English that marks him as coming from a rural or unread group.

2 But if he doesn't mind being so marked, there's no reason why he should change.

3 Samuel Johnson kept a Staffordshire burr in his speech all his life.

3 In Burns mouth the despised lowland Scots dialect served just as well as the correct English spoken by ten million of his southern contemporaries.

3 Lincoln's vocabulary and his way of pronouncing certain words were sneered at by many better educated people at the time, but he seemed to be able to use the English language as effectively as his critics.

This structure is represented (and emphasized) by the following diagram, in which the numbers represent the sequence, not levels, of T-units.

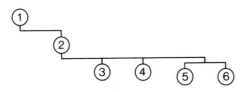

As the passages being analyzed get longer, such a drawing becomes much more efficient than recopying the whole passage; it also demonstrates the pattern more vividly.

Sequence is indicated both by the numbers in the circles and by the movement from left to right. Level of generality is indicated by the relative height of the circles. Logical (modifying) relationships are indicated by the lines that connect the circles. If a writer puts an irrelevant statement in the middle of a passage (as sentence 3 of the following example), the lack of connection is indicated by the lack of lines.

(1) One American Indian tribe, the Iroquois, consider themselves a nation apart from the United States, even though they are citizens. (2) When the United States declared war on Germany in 1917, the Iroquois sent a message to Washington that they too had declared war. (3) They intended to use bows and arrows, though. (4) Since Germany made no separate peace treaty with the Iroquois at the end of World War I, the Iroquois didn't think it necessary to declare war again in 1941. (5) Some other Indian tribes also think of themselves as separate nations.

The second sentence is a proof: it gives a reason for believing the first. The syllogism behind the enthymeme is:

Only nations can declare war.
The Iroquois declared war.
Therefore, the Iroquois consider themselves a nation.

Although the third sentence of the passage seems to be related to the second, it is actually functionally irrelevant, not on topic, not part of an idea string; in Markels' terms, we have an equivalence chain (*Iroquois, Iroquois, They*), but not "an acceptable inference chain" consistent with the topic sentence ("Cohesion Paradigms" 460). The fourth sentence is coordinate with the second. Although the first sentence is the topic sentence of the paragraph, the fifth asserts an encompassing generalization (what the first sentence says about *one* tribe the fifth says about *some* tribes). Thus even if we exclude the irrelevant sentence, this paragraph contains three levels of generality; and, interestingly, the topic sentence is not the highest level of generality. The matrix drawing of the passage looks like this:

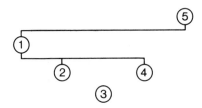

Note that the lines show 5 as superordinate to *1* (not to *4*) and that no line is drawn to *3*, thus indicating its logical irrelevance.

The Nold and Davis matrix uses lines redundantly to represent sequence; using lines to represent the relationships of the T-units has several advantages. It allows the matrix to represent cases in which a T-unit logically relates not to the immediately preceding T-unit but to one elsewhere in the passage; thus when a writer starts a new (sub)topic, the matrix can indicate where that new (sub)topic connects to an earlier part of the discourse—which is more significant than its apparent relationship, or lack of relationship, to the immediately preceding T-unit. It also allows the matrix to indicate that a particular T-unit logically relates to *several* other T-units, which is especially useful in analyzing both very sophisticated and very unsophisticated writing.

The lines represent various logical distinctions: whether a superordinate T-unit represents a change of subject or a conclusion drawn from a preceding series of T-units; whether a T-unit has no logical relationship with those preceding and following it (as in poorly composed discourse); whether two T-units function as one item in a string (as the last two T-units on page 35 above); and so forth.

Ambiguities

When doing a discourse matrix, as in most such analyses, it is important to count as a sentence (or T-unit or clause) any clearly complete statement—i.e., to accept ellipsis. Thus a single word, such as "No," may be a complete unit:

Does it mean the guidance of the party is no longer needed?
No.

Here "No" is clearly an ellipsis for "No, it does not mean that." The writer's clear intent, the rhetorical function, and the normal reader's response all converge to justify counting this single word as a complete statement. This is the same principle that English teachers have traditionally used for defining "acceptable" sentence fragments.

A quotation within a text—and especially within a sentence—should generally be treated as a single T-unit, "So-and-so stated, 'x.'" Sometimes, however, the statements in the quotation are so integral to the text that they must be analyzed as part of the text. (Whether a quotation is thus integral to the text depends to some extent upon the reader's interpretation.)

It is important to remember that texts may be ambiguous: there may be more than one correct way to perceive the relationship of a given statement to the discourse in which it appears. Certain apparent ambiguities, however, can be resolved. When there seems to be a contradiction between what is indicated by comparison of levels of generality out of communicative context and what is indicated by analysis of modification or functional/rhetorical relationship (in communicative context), one should give priority to the latter. When in doubt, it is important to remember that analysis must be based not just on close examination of a few adjacent statements, but on functional semantic relationships within the discourse, relationships that are sometimes ambiguous until context is considered. That is to say, the matrix is used to analyze not bits of language but discourse, i.e., language in context. For meaning, as I. A. Richards emphasizes, is contextual.

Classification may be confirmed by looking at conjuncts and other cohesion cues used by the writer to mark these relationships, although it must be remembered that writers do not always mark them accurately, that "surface structure" cues in general are thus indicators, not proofs, of "deep structure." Subordination is often marked by inclusive conjuncts (e.g., *for example*), coordination by sequential, coordinative, contrastive, or alternative conjuncts (e.g., *then, furthermore, however, or*), superordination by causal or conclusory conjuncts (e.g., *therefore, so*).[14]

Sloan points out three reasons to be cautious about relying on conjuncts to clarify such classifications. First, he argues convincingly that these seven types of conjuncts do not constitute a comprehensive system. Second, he points out that conjuncts sometimes signal relationships between subordinate elements, not "between the *total* content" of T-units. Third, he demonstrates that ambiguous conjuncts are commonplace. Sloan does assert, nonetheless, that the "principal value" of explicit markers is to guide readers to interpret potentially ambiguous passages as the writer would. ("Transitions," esp. 452)

W. Ross Winterowd, in "The Grammar of Coherence," also makes the point that "there can be ambiguity in transitions as well as in lexicon and syntax" (231). The following example contains two such ambiguities.

(1) There is an amazement proper to the experience of all great art, (2) but the special amazement which *War and Peace* revives in me while I am reading it is like that of a child. (3) The child does not expect the unexpected; (4) that would already be a preparation against it. (5) He does not for an instant doubt that a certain event had to happen; (6) such a doubt obscures. (7) He may even have been told beforehand that it was going to happen; (8) such foreknowledge is as little a part of him as a label in his cap. (9) He is able to look at the thing itself. (10) The event reaches him radiant with magical causes but not yet trapped in sufficient cause. (11) Tolstoy does not, as many do, achieve this freshness by transforming the reading into a never-never land. (12) On the contrary his fictional mode is realistic; (13) the people in his novel appear and behave like possible people in the world we daily live in. (14) His achievement is the greater because he uses the mode of realism, (15) for realism offers a threat to which other literary modes are not subject, the encroachment of mediocrity.

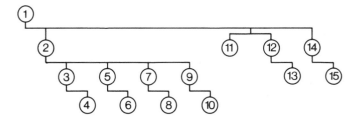

This passage, originally chosen by Karrfalt and later reanalyzed by Nold and Davis (see appendix B), contains two significant ambiguities. It is possible to read the opening two T-units as coordinate, i.e., as contrasting two types of amazement; indeed, perhaps because they believe *contrast* is always a coordinate relationship, that is how Nold and Davis did read it. It is also possible, in my view preferable, to read them as statements about amazement in general and the amazement provoked by *War and Peace* in particular, in which case the second is subordinate to the first. The writer's choice of the coordinating conjunction *but* seems to validate the first reading. Out of context, however, one would certainly judge the first T-unit more general than the second. And there is a standard sort of introduction in which a general principle is stated by way of introducing an exceptional case that is the writer's actual subject. Christensen, in fact, discussed as special cases such paragraphs with introductory transitions or comparisons that, as he put it, "do not belong to the sequence," i.e., are not part of the topic encompassed by the paragraph ("Paragraph" 153–54); but such cases are so common that to treat them as "special" is really to avoid the issue. (For Karrfalt, by the by, this particular ambiguity did not arise because he dealt with sentences, not T-units.)

The relationship between T-units 9 and *10* is similarly ambiguous. The semicolons that connect *3* to *4*, *5* to *6*, and *7* to *8* are succeeded by a period between *9* and *10*. That shifting cohesion cue may be taken to indicate that *9* and *10* have a different relationship than the preceding three pairs, that they are coordinate. I take it, however, as a kind of emphasis, as an indication that *9–10* is not just another item on the list but rather the most important item, to which the list is building.[15]

The crucial point is that, by definition, a matrix drawing is a schematic representation of a reader's understanding of a text. If one reader reads the text accurately while another misreads it, then we can say that the second reader's matrix is wrong. But if a text is ambiguous and several readers reach distinct but valid understandings, then those readers would draw different matrixes—and all would be correct. Taken as a group, these different but correct matrixes accurately represent the ambiguity of the text.

In communicative context, ambiguity often does not matter because the shift in emphasis may be so slight that it does not produce significantly distinct meanings. Where it does yield several distinct readings, and hence several matrix drawings of a single passage, some empiricists may see the resulting polysemy as a problem. But the only "solution" to the "problem" would be to abolish ambiguous texts. In short, what appears to be a problem with the matrix is actually an accurate representation of a quality of texts: ambiguity.

Despite inevitable difficulties caused by ambiguity in the meaning of texts, matrix analysis helps us to explicate and diagram relationships among levels of generality, which are "at the heart of all discourse" and "central to concept formation" (Berthoff, "Intelligent Eye" 196). Though less than a complete "grammar of passages," the discourse matrix is one important key to such a "grammar," perhaps even the most important. Although the instrument presumably still needs some refining, it has considerable power to generate interesting insights and effective pedagogies, as the following chapter will indicate.

4

Applications

The challenge to experimental design is not to dispense with meaning. . . . If college students find generalizing difficult, it's because nobody has ever taught them how to go about it, and abstraction which proceeds by means of generalizing—*concept formation*, as it is often called—must be deliberately learned and should therefore be deliberately taught.

—Ann Berthoff ("Is Teaching Still Possible?" 747, 753–54)

MY RESEARCH COLLABORATORS AND I HAVE DISCOVERED, OR sometimes stumbled upon, a wide range of uses for the discourse matrix. We have used the matrix to investigate with controlled precision a variety of structures we used to grasp more intuitively. We have used it in contrastive rhetoric, particularly to contrast certain standard structures of Chinese and English discourses. We have used it also in teaching, to help students learn particular structures, to help them locate the inadequacies of poor structure, to teach advanced concepts in punctuation, to provide students with concepts that unify various material we used to present piecemeal, and to enable them to undertake their own investigations of specific structures they wish to master.

Some of the descriptive and pedagogical studies that follow are the result of appropriately controlled, reliable, valid empirical research. Others are at best pilot studies, suggestive of hypotheses worth investigating more carefully, but grounds for drawing only the most qualified and tentative conclusions. The reason for presenting these studies here is not to make definitive assertions about English paragraphing, the rhetorical structure of Chinese discourse, effective teaching, or any other such matter; rather, they are presented as evidence of the descriptive and pedagogical potential of the discourse matrix. The primary purpose is to encourage further research that might allow definitive conclusions about various important and fascinating matters.

The nature of composition as an applied discipline is such, however, that as teachers we are unable to wait for the completion and replication of definitive research. "Monday morning" often arrives before the relevant research has been completed, let alone reported and replicated. When qualified by practical experience and informed intuition, even limited research is better than prejudice as a basis for teaching. Fortunately, even some of the unconfirmed hypotheses generated by discourse matrix theory, such as hypotheses about punctuation, seem to work for our students. This, of course, is one of the reasons our discipline needs theory as well as research—indeed, needs theory to frame research.

Standard Structures

Properly socialized members of a rhetorical community share tacit understanding of the appropriate arrangement of statements within a communication—an understanding they may not be able to articulate in detail, especially with regard to detailed structure within nameable parts of the discourse (cf. Reid). Any distinct culture is, of course, a unique rhetorical community. To a lesser extent, this proposition is true for distinct historical periods of a particular culture, for subcultures, or even for distinct types of discourse within a particular subculture at a particular time.

Most English teachers, however, can say little about structuring statements within a paragraph beyond asserting that there is almost always a controlling generalization, often articulated as a topic sentence, and "support." Generally, they do not even recognize that "support" is a physical (probably architectural) metaphor, suggesting that a generalization is somehow like a roof beam, which needs to be held up by lower-level structures. Nor do they usually have a historical understanding which might allow them to recognize why such a metaphor and the structure it implies should be generally preferred in cultures dominated by empirical science, with its emphasis on inductive reasoning. Certainly they do not often question the validity of drawing an analogy between ideas and physical structures (nor consider, within the analogy, the intriguing possibility that one idea might be cantilevered off another, or hung from the ceiling, not supported from below). It is not surprising, therefore, that the empirical research has not been done which would allow us to state for a given type of discourse precisely what the most common patterns are, let alone to theorize about why and how those patterns function in their normal discourse contexts.

Our matrix analysis of English paragraph structure and other standard structures began, as it happens, in China. For in China, as in most developing countries, teachers cannot depend on the intuitive grasp of such structures that we have come to expect from many Western students, i.e., from those who have the "right" sort of background, those whose parents are members of university-educated subcultures (cf. Matalene, Min-zhao Lu). In China, as in North American basic writing classes for native speakers of English, the inadequacy of our descriptive instruments is exceptionally obvious. And adequate description often enables effective teaching.

When Is a Paragraph?

Although we have long known that the paragraphing practices of competent writers only sometimes correspond with the Platonic ideal advocated dogmatically by most composition textbooks—Richard Braddock's oft-cited study of topic sentences, published in 1974, provided dramatic empirical verification—we do not yet have an adequate theory of paragraphing; nor, beyond the oft-investigated issue of the frequency and placement of topic sentences, do we know much about the internal structure of paragraphs. These two contradictions—(1) between textbook "theory" and writers' actual practices and (2) between what we need to know and what we actually do know—create problems in the classroom. And these problems are often exacerbated because teachers are not conscious of the contradictions they unwittingly present to their students.

Seeking to expose such contradictions, Zhu Wei-fang, Lu Zheng-wei, Xu Yong-hui, and Long Won-guang used the matrix to examine the structure of prose in anthologies they were assigned to teach. Zhu, for example, examined the semantic structure of selections from Wu et al., *Readings in Modern English Prose*, essays that were regarded as students' models in a reading and writing course at the Beijing Foreign Language Institute. Her study (1982) was designed

1. to find out to what extent this type of discourse actually uses semantically unified, topic-sentence-first paragraphs,
2. to find out when "conceptual" paragraphs or stadia/superordinations are signalled by indentations and when by other devices,
3. to hypothesize a functional explanation for the structures she discovered.

The scope of her study did not enable Zhu to make generalizations about English prose structure, not even within a particular genre. It did, however, allow her to make her own empirical observations instead of relying on the dogmatic assertions of traditional English composition textbooks. It allowed her to discover that the exemplars she was giving her English composition students contradicted the textbook rule for paragraph development she was teaching them— to discover, in short, that the exemplars did not exemplify.

In analyzing passages, each three physical paragraphs long, randomly selected from each of nine selections—i.e., a total of twenty-seven paragraphs written by the like of J. B. S. Haldane, Bertrand Russell, John Kenneth Galbraith, and James Baldwin—Zhu found only six proper topic-sentence-first paragraphs and only seven more where the physical paragraph (i.e., indentation) matched the conceptual paragraph (i.e., semantic unity). In seven more cases, the physical paragraph contined two or more high-level generalizations. And the last seven physical paragraphs turned out to contain only three conceptual paragraphs (i.e., there were one or two indentations within what would have been a single textbook paragraph—or, to put it the other way round, a single topic sentence was developed through two or three physical paragraphs).

Although Zhu's experience indicates a potential use for the matrix in teacher training, what she discovered about topic sentences is new only in the sense that her sample was composed entirely of paragraphs being presented to students as exemplars. But the matrix also enabled her to look at other aspects of the internal structure of these paragraphs. Only four paragraphs could be described simply as *generalization plus specifics* (i.e., as topic sentence plus *specific* "support"). Thirteen of the paragraphs contained three levels of generality, while six more contained four levels. Of the fifty-six superordinations she found in these twenty-seven physical paragraphs, only eighteen (32 percent) were signaled by indentations and only eleven (20 percent) by transition words. Twenty more were identifiable from their phrasing as sentences of judgment, conclusion, or generalization (i.e., part of the preceding stadium, as defined by Rodgers), and the remaining seven were marked by no obvious signal. When a logical relationship is obvious there may be no need for a conjunct or other cohesion cue, but textbook treatments of "transitions" rarely deal with this commonsensical understanding.

If one defines an ideal paragraph psycholinguistically, i.e., as one which may be read most efficiently because it is semantically unified and states its main proposition in the first sentence, there were only seven ideal paragraphs in Zhu's sample of twenty-seven paragraphs. She had to conclude, therefore, that this textbook pattern is only one way of relating sentences, that mature writers relate their sentences in various ways in accordance with rhetorical and semantic contexts. Her findings tend to confirm Rodgers' hypothesis that a new stadium represents an option to indent, which a writer may or may not take; the instances in which indentations occurred at places other than superordinations, however, raises questions about both Rodgers' implied hypothesis that indentations ordinarily occur *only* where stadia begin and Christensen's definition of a paragraph.

All the writers in Zhu's sample did seem to use patterns grounded in a single basic cognitive principle: inductive logic. This is consistent with the hypothesis that English stadia and paragraphs are characterized by patterns of subordination which reflect the dominance of empirical scientific thinking in Anglo-American discourse. These inductive patterns are based on a discourse rule that generalizations should be supported by particulars (or more narrowly, that opinions should be supported by facts). Among the set of inductive patterns available, a preference for the one in which the "point" is stated explicitly in the first sentence may be ascribed, in part, to a scientific skepticism: if readers know from the start what (hypo)thesis is being asserted, they are better able to evaluate the supporting arguments critically.

Although the dominance of inductive patterns is typical of modernized industrial societies, it is quite contrary to the dominant patterns of feudal societies, and its place in the discourses of tribal/ gathering societies is a rather more complex question (Needham, chap. 10, esp. 86–131). Zhu's research suggests that there may be in English a greater variety of rhetorical patterns based on induction than the English composition textbooks discuss. If true, this would create an especial difficulty for students from cultures that put a lesser emphasis on inductive patterns to begin with.

Some of the simpler complexities uncovered by the research of Zhu, Lu, Xu, and Long are well illustrated by the following example:

(1) A topic sentence at the beginning of a paragraph can help both readers and writers. (2) Readers benefit most. (3) Their attention is focussed immediately, (4) and they can see the argument develop. (5) Writers benefit indirectly. (6) When they write, they can keep their reasoning clear and explicit. (7) They can also avoid digressions, as when a short controlling sentence at the beginning of a list narrows the choices a writer can make when completing the list. (8) Thus a topic sentence that opens the paragraph is a useful tool for a writer.

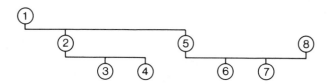

This simple paragraph contains two stadia, the second of which begins with T-unit 5. Because the two stadia are short and controlled by a single generalization (T-unit *1*), they would in most contexts be formatted as a single paragraph. If, however, the stadia were developed at greater length (such that each was "long enough"), they would in most contexts be presented as two paragraphs. Stadia, as Rodgers emphasized, *may be*, but do not have to be demarcated by paragraph indentations.

There are two points to be made about this example. The first is that most textbooks have nothing to say about this structure and the paragraphing decision it presents. How is a composition student (or anyone who does not already understand the principle, at least tacitly) to decide when to present such a structure as a single paragraph and when as two paragraphs? The second point follows from the typical overgeneralization of students who are beginning to master this structure. If they decide to start a new paragraph for the second stadium (T-unit 5), they often go back and indent between the generalization (which controls *both* subtopics) and the first subtopic—in this case between T-units *1* and *2*. In terms of logic, parallelism, and symmetry, this additional indentation makes sense; the problem is that it violates the norms of the discourse community. But most textbooks say nothing about paragraphing that could help these students qualify their overgeneralization. (For an even more interesting example, see the Bertrand Russell paragraph analyzed in appendix B.)

While hardly far-reaching enough to allow definitive statements about paragraphing in English, these studies, together with those reported below, demonstrate the power of the discourse matrix as an instrument for investigating paragraph structure and its effectiveness as a basis for teaching that structure. (For some hypotheses about how competent writers of modern English prose make their paragraphing decisions, see appendix C.)

Specialized Discourses

The same techniques that are used to identify the rhetorical patterns of a culture may be used to identify the patterns of a particular discourse within a culture. One example of using the discourse matrix to analyze the structure of a specialized discourse in preparation for teaching is provided by Ning Yi-zhong. Not surprisingly, Ning discovered that in newsmagazines such as *Time* and *Newsweek* indentations (physical paragraphs) occur much more frequently than do stadia. In one sample of thirty-two physical paragraphs, he found only fifteen stadia. He also found that stadia typically contained only two levels of generality (although stadia with one or three levels were not uncommon) and that topic sentences were more often implied than overt. The traditional conception of an English paragraph, he had to conclude, seems not to apply to this type of discourse. Moreover, as Eden and Mitchell point out, thus emphasizing how conventional such structures are, had Ning looked at nineteenth-century newspapers from the United States, he probably would have discovered a contrary pattern—indentations occurring much *less* frequently than stadia (418).

This sort of analysis of a specialized discourse could be just as useful to someone trying to learn to write like a lawyer or an engineer. It is especially useful to someone desiring to become a free-lance writer (or to anyone who wants to know how to write *in general*, not to master just essay writing or technical writing or journalism). A writer wanting to write for a particular type of magazine might ask what sorts of paragraphs predominate in such magazines, how many levels of generality they typically contain, in which patterns, using which types of subordination. One student, for example, having examined *Quill and Quire*, reported that "the typical paragraph is structured so that the sentence with the lowest level of generality comes first. In addition, the article as a whole typically becomes more general towards its conclusion."[16]

Pedagogy

The same sort of analysis can be used by teachers. For example, the discourse matrix has been used by Susan Fahey in teaching the rudiments of technical writing to engineering technology students at a postsecondary institute. She needed to know what sorts of paragraph structures are most common in writing about engineering and how best to convey those structures to her students. Her empirical study provides remarkably significant statistical evidence of the matrix's pedagogical effectiveness.

Fahey's specific experimental goal was to teach the technical writer's list, one of the most common patterns of technical writing aimed at technical audiences, so she began by verifying the commonness of the pattern and its specific description ("An Analysis of Technical Writing"). This pattern requires an opening generalization which frames the list, plus a number of list-items, each of which is specifically developed. An opening generalization is not the "point" so much as it is a frame which "holds" and labels the more specific information. A conclusion or regeneralization at the end is, therefore, inappropriate. Drawn as a matrix, the pattern looks like this:

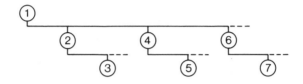

(There may, of course, be more than three idea strings and more than one T-unit per string at the lowest level.)

Fahey introduced the concept of levels of generality to her class and did some exercises to make sure the students had grasped it. She then showed the students how to do a simple matrix analysis and how to use the pattern explicated through that analysis as a pattern for invention, a form to be filled. She tried to concretize the concept through analogy: with students specializing in electronic technology, for example, she redrew the technical writer's list matrix as an electric circuit such that a single missing T-unit would break the circuit (and cause the light bulb at the end not to light). A colleague teaching nursing students made the same point by using a diagram of hospital administrative structure as the analogy.

The students' reaction was extremely positive—basically, "Oh, so that's what you want. Why didn't you tell us before?" In a pilot study, under examination conditions, thirteen of twenty students in the experimental group correctly reproduced the pattern (in contrast with zero of twenty in the control group). Since the pilot study indicated that the discourse matrix is a potentially powerful pedagogy, Fahey replicated the study with more rigorous controls and quantifications.

The second experiment involved two experienced lecturers, an inexperienced teaching assistant, an independent, experienced matrix analyst, and 136 electrical engineering technology students at a two-year technical institute. Both lecturers set out to teach the technical writer's list. Lecturer T, a traditional instructor, explained unity and coherence, demonstrated the function and placement of topic sentences and transitions, showed many models of good technical paragraphs, and discussed why they were good. Lecturer M, using a pedagogy based on the discourse matrix, lectured about levels of generality, coordination, subordination, and superordination, the placement and level of topic sentences, and the matrix representation of technical paragraphs. (This contrast may indicate something about the efficacy of using models to teach structure, for Lecturer M gave a detailed description of the desired structure, while Lecturer T, relying on less specific terminology, defined the structure less fully and then relied on the students' ability to intuit it from the models.)

The two lecturers also supervised tutorials based on their own respective pedagogical methods. Other tutorials were run by a teaching assistant, who used the model, vocabulary, and feedback techniques of whichever lecturer the students in that particular tutorial had heard; thus the teaching assistant, who did not know she was part of a study until after all data had been collected, served as a neutral instructor, a control for instructor bias.

The students were given pretest writing assignments before the course started; on their midterm, several weeks after the relevant instruction, the questions were reversed, each group writing on the topics assigned to the other in the pretest. The independent, experienced matrix analyst (a research assistant) then drew a matrix for each paragraph without knowing which instructional group the writer was from and without knowing whether the sample was a pretest or a posttest. From the matrix, he coded each paragraph according to five criteria relevant to this particular technical paragraph structure:

1. The first T-unit should be the most general.
2. Each T-unit should be relevant to both the preceding superordinate T-unit and to the topic sentence.
3. The paragraph should contain at least three idea strings and at least three levels of generality.
4. Each idea string should be developed by coordination and subordination only.
5. There should be *no* regeneralization at the end (i.e., no return to the level of generality of the opening T-unit).

Statistical analysis showed that the matrix group scored higher than the traditional instruction group on all five criteria. The two groups of students were statistically equivalent before instruction started; though both groups showed some improvement, the matrix group was significantly superior after instruction. Analysis of data from only those students supervised by the neutral instructor clearly demonstrated that the difference was created by the method of instruction, not by the instructor.

In terms of the specific criteria, both teaching methods were demonstrably effective in increasing the number of paragraphs that opened with a topic sentence, and the difference between the two methods was not statistically significant. Both groups also produced more relevant T-units after instruction, with the matrix group scoring somewhat higher; but the two groups had not been equivalent by this particular criteria on the pretest so no statistically significant conclusions could be drawn in this regard. After instruction, the matrix group produced more idea strings while the traditional instruction group actually produced fewer—possibly because traditional instruction includes no terminology for discussing and emphasizing this characteristic. The matrix group also became more successful at explaining, exemplifying, or otherwise developing their ideas, while the traditional instruction group again actually did worse on the posttest (i.e., they produced fewer coordinate and subordinate T-units after instruction than they had before instruction). The matrix group was also significantly better on the posttest at avoiding the closing regeneralization, which is inappropriate to this type of technical discourse.[17]

In total, the matrix group improved their scores and achieved higher scores than the traditional instruction group on all characteristics tested, and significantly higher scores on three. The traditional instruction group achieved higher scores on three characteristics while actually declining on the other two. In all cases, the scores of students supervised by the neutral instructor demonstrated that the teaching method, not the instructor, was the significant variable. Fahey concluded that the matrix method is superior in every way examined by the study and that traditional instruction actually distracts students from the detailed and appropriate development of their ideas.

Fahey's studies, while confined to a particular type of writing and a particular type of student, indicate the pedagogical potential of the matrix. Like various techniques teachers have long used—such as clustering activities, "mind mapping," even outlining—the matrix calls students' attention to development and organization, but it does so with much more precision, fullness, and power. It also has the virtue of providing a visual explanation for a verbal phenomenon.

Contrastive Rhetoric

When foreign students write English compositions they are likely to be influenced somehow by their native "patterns of thought flow" (Rodgers, "Stadium of Discourse" 178) or by their traditional rhetorical patterns. The result of this influence is that, even if they know how to use words accurately and structure sentences correctly, they may fail to use rhetorical patterns which will be easily recognized by native English readers. To make these assertions is merely to assume, in keeping with the rhetorical tradition from Isocrates through Burke, that language learning and socialization are interrelated processes (if not two aspects of one process), that culture influences the linguistic and rhetorical forms an individual learns. Cross-cultural communication is, therefore, likely to involve conflicts between the distinct frames and forms of the different cultures. And as Robert Bander asserts, "An awareness that rhetorical patterns differ from one culture to another can help [students of composition] become more quickly proficient in a writing pattern that is not native to them" (4).

Contrastive rhetoric allows teachers to show their students the structural differences between culturally distinct discourses. This helps students know which of their own culture's patterns are readily readable in the foreign discourse. It also helps teachers know which foreign patterns are new to their classes and therefore need to be practiced. Though the following discussion emphasizes contrasts between cultures, the underlying principle should also be applicable to contrasts between subcultures or discourse communities (cf. Reither, Bruffee). Indeed, Patricia Bizzell specifically hypothesizes that what happens when basic writers come to university may be analogous to what happens when someone enters a foreign culture.

The differences between the cultural contexts of Chinese and English are extraordinary in themselves and are compounded by the cognitive differences between the thought structures dominant in modernized and traditional societies. If the Chinese are to communicate effectively with Westerners, or even to interpret Western texts correctly, they need to learn those rhetorical structures that reflect the dominance of inductive cognitive structures in modern scientific and professional contexts. The dominance of these structures is not at all "natural"—indeed, they were not dominant in Western cultures prior to the rise of modern science (cf. the dominant cognitive structures of medieval scholastic texts).

Robert Kaplan suggests that Chinese students have difficulty keeping their English compositions coherent because of the difference between the direct lineal structure of English discourse and what he posits as the "spiraling" structure of culturally typical Chinese discourse.[18] He argues, in effect, that Aristotle's "available means" of communication is a culturally defined category. The discourse matrix was used by Jia Shan, Sun-I Chen, and Irene Hessami to test this hypothesis.

Looking at Chinese composition textbooks, which teach such rhetorical patterns as comparison/contrast, classification, definition, analogy, exemplification, process analysis, and causal explanation, Jia found little reason to expect significant differences between Chinese and English paragraph structure. After drawing matrixes of Chinese essays by Lu Xun, Mao Ze-dung, and Zhou En-lai, however, Jia suggested that there are two types of paragraphs in Chinese, one much like an inductive English paragraph, another resembling what Kaplan titles an "Oriental" spiral. An empirical examination of her sample texts had turned up a number of paragraphs (three of seventeen in Mao's "Things Are Beginning to Change," for example) where matrix analysis suggested this non-English pattern. To communicate effectively with Chinese, or even to interpret Chinese texts correctly, Westerners need to learn to recognize this pattern.

These non-English paragraphs seem to reflect a Chinese rhetorical pattern—formalized, for example, in the traditional eight-part essay—of presenting an idea in a repetitive yet developing spiral. An eight-part essay begins by asserting the importance of the topic; the next three parts develop aspects of the topic, the fifth and sixth parts develop these same aspects further; then the concluding two parts repeat the main theme. Generally known in English as the "eight-legged" essay, although that is a somewhat strange translation, this rhetorical form pretty much died out in the late nineteenth century along with the Imperial examination system. Although the eight-part essay is an archaic form, a kind of "school essay" used primarily on examinations, the underlying rhetorical principles remain part of Chinese culture. Direct influence on modern Chinese writing is improbable, but the eight-part essay reflects a habitual mode of thought also reflected in certain modern Chinese passages.

Thus in one long paragraph (twenty-three T-units), Mao seems through the first nine T-units to be developing his topic by division much as an English writer might. He tells his readers that there are various types of Party members; he then names three types, elaborating on each briefly. But then he returns to the second type, and then to the third type. Several T-units later, he makes the same returns again. Toward the end of the paragraph, he returns to discuss the second type before concluding that low-level cadres should not be given an undue share of the blame for the errors committed by these last two types.

When Chinese paragraphs of this kind are translated into English, they certainly look misorganized and "illogical" to native English readers (though it is worth noting that they might not have looked so alien to native English readers some centuries ago). They fly in the face of Nold and Davis' second constraint: "Once the T-unit chain has left a stadium, it may *never* return to it" (149), i.e., once a subtopic has been discussed and passed, one should not return to it.

Although Chinese students are quick to learn how to write certain standard English paragraphs (since these patterns are part of their own culture's discourse), Jia hypothesizes that, when they write compositions considered by their English instructors to be illogical and to contain irrelevancies, they are sometimes using this other Chinese structure without realizing that most English readers will not recognize it. If they were taught the distinctions between Chinese and English discourse, they could avoid using "Chinese-only" patterns in their English writing, thus communicating more effectively.

Contrastive rhetoric using discourse matrix analysis suggests a way of improving composition instruction in foreign languages, and perhaps also of improving instruction for native speakers moving from one subculture, discipline, or discourse community to another. It also suggests that the basis of Nold and Davis' second constraint may be ethnocentric insofar as there is any implication that the constraint applies to all writing, not just to certain types of modern Western discourse.

Two studies by Chen are similarly suggestive. In a pilot project, "A Comparative Analysis of Paragraph Structures in Chinese and English," Chen examined paragraph structure in academic philosophy journals, contrasting articles written in English by native speakers of English, in English by native speakers of Chinese, and in Chinese by native speakers of Chinese. Matrix analysis revealed clear distinctions between the English and Chinese of native speakers; not surprisingly, English written by native speakers of Chinese seemed to compromise between the two native-speaker patterns.

Despite the inherent conciseness of the Chinese language, the Chinese paragraphs (like premodern English paragraphs, I suspect) contained many more T-units (averaging 13.3 T-units, while the English averaged 7.5). While the longest English paragraphs by native speakers contained eighteen T-units, the longest native English paragraph by a Chinese speaker contained twenty-four, and several Chinese paragraphs exceeded thirty. Fully 23 percent of the Chinese paragraphs exceeded eighteen T-units (i.e., almost a quarter of the Chinese paragraphs were longer than the longest English paragraph in the sample). The Chinese paragraphs also tended to include both more levels of generality and longer node strings; eight of thirty Chinese paragraphs had longer node strings than any English paragraph by a native speaker.

Most of the English paragraphs in this sample, unlike Braddock's, began with topic sentences, and they often ended with concluding sentences. Aside from a number of very short transition paragraphs, the Chinese paragraphs tended to have the highest level of generality (often a topic sentence) near the middle or end. The Chinese paragraphs also tended to cover more subtopics. Thus the Chinese paragraphs had more stadia per physical paragraph.

Here is a typically long paragraph, translated rather literally, from a Chinese philosophical journal (divided into T-units in accordance with the Chinese text):

(1) Concluding from the discussion above, *I Ching* [the Book of Changes] was a cooperative work written through a long period of time. (2) This book is different from *The Poems, The Document* , and the "Tze" type of books, which are based on one single philosopher's thoughts. (3) The former two were cooperative works, (4) but they were not based on a particular topic. (5) *The Poems* consisted of the poems of the Shang and Chou dynasties. (6) *The Document* is the collection of the governmental literature of the Tang, Yu, Shia, Shang, and Chou dynasties. (7) *I Ching*, on the other hand, was not a literary work, nor governmental literature, but a work of fortune telling. (8) Seen as based on a central problem, it is quite like the "Tze" type of books; (9) for instance, *Chuang-tze* consisted of three parts. (10) The last two parts were not written by Chung-tze himself, but is a collection of essays about him. (11) These essays were all based on Chuang-tze's principles, (12) and the discussions were explanations surrounding the concepts proposed by Chuang-tze. (13) Another example, *Mo-tze*, is quite similar too. (14) It was not written by Mo-tze himself either, but by his followers. (15) However, there must be a basis in a person's thoughts for his followers' further development. (16) *I Ching* was not developed from a person's thought, but from a topic. (17) The essence of this topic seemed to be religious, (18) but it did not develop into a religion, as Christianity and Buddhism did, but into aspects of communication between God and man in ancient China. (19) There are different explanations about how the communication is achieved. (20) For example, in Christianity, oracles were directly given by God through prophets or priests; (21) similarly in ancient Chinese literature, God sometimes communicated directly with the rulers. (22) But according to *Chia-gu Pu-te* of the Yin dynasty, man learned God's will by casting lots instead of directly from God. (23) The "eight symbols" was also a medium for communication. (24) This kind of communication is only part of a religion, (25) but in Chou dynasty a complicated system casting lots was developed from it. (26) And from the casting lots system, a philosophical apprehension was developed. (27) Furthermore, on this basis, explanation of the origin of everything, the relationships between heaven and man, the significance of life, was developed. (28) This explanation was not a denial of the existing religious concept, but a combination of religion and philosophy. (29) Consequently, the development of the *I Ching* was not like Christianity, which never extended beyond religious aspects, rather it was more like that of Dionysianism in ancient Greece. (30) Dionysianism, according to contemporary research, was established

on the ideology of lower class people, who had given up hope for the earthly world. (31) However, when it was combined with Pythagoreanism, the religousness turned into a mathematical philosophy, which was based on human apprehension. (32) This philosophy did not deny the original religion, but coexisted with it.

However one might analyze this paragraph, it clearly is not constrained as tightly and concisely to the linear development of a controlling topic as one would expect in English.

Chen's second study was a comparable but more rigorous analysis of English and Chinese editorials from both communist and capitalist newspapers, designed to investigate what matrix analysis might reveal about cultural and political influences on rhetorical patterns. She also hypothesized that the T-unit might not take into account certain structural differences between English and Chinese, so she used the clause, not the T-unit, as the basis of her analysis.[19] (She also hoped to discover something about the importance or unimportance of subordinate clauses to the structure of intersentence rhetorical patterns.)

Chen found that both cultural and political factors correlated significantly with the structure of the discourse in these editorials. Surprisingly, however, no significant interaction was found between cultural and political influences on discourse structure. Culture seemed to influence primarily the overall structure, while political stance influenced primarily how development occurred within that larger structure.

Both node strings and idea strings were significantly longer in the Chinese editorials, indicating more high-level parallel structures (roughly stated, more subtopics and/or restatement) and more clauses used to develop each subtopic. But despite using more clauses to develop a subtopic, Chinese editorials used fewer, though not significantly fewer, levels of generality. That is, the fuller development did not involve increased specificity, as one might expect in English; rather, it seemed to involve increased redundancy of one sort or another. This is as one might expect: the more a culture has been influenced by empiricism and a predominance of inductive reasoning, the more convincing are discourse patterns that emphasize development through specificity. The depth of development (number of levels of generality) was greatest in an English-language communist newspaper, *The Guardian*, and lowest in a Chinese-language capitalist newspaper, *Chung-Yang.*

Unlike language, political stance did not correlate significantly with the number of node strings used in an editorial, and lack of homogeneity in the sample prevented statistically reliable conclusions about its correlation with number of levels of generality or number of idea strings. Political stance did, however, correlate significantly with the number of subtopics and subordinate clauses within a node string and with the number of levels of generality within an idea string. The communist editorials had more parallel subtopics under a generalization and used more clauses to elaborate a subtopic. The communist newspapers (with the exception of *The Guardian*) seemed to use much more repetition for emphasis, especially when urging readers to adopt a certain attitude or take a particular action. The capitalist newspapers, however, used more levels of generality in developing a subtopic, indicating more reliance on inductive validation by giving specific details.[20]

Like Jia, Chen concluded that there is in Chinese discourse a tendency which sometimes produces what Westerners perceive as a meandering or spiraling pattern. She noted that a conclusion drawn in the middle of a paragraph is often further developed or becomes the basis for a new subtopic.

Chen, Jia, and I hypothesize that this pattern may have a basis in traditional Chinese composition. Like the other liberal arts, composition in ancient China was a means of moral education. A spiraling repetition of the central idea through various comparisons (similes, metaphors, allegories) may have been valued because of its didactic function. The skillful use of comparisons, including indirect reference to classical texts, certainly also had an ethical function in Aristotle's sense, demonstrating the speaker's or writer's knowledge and technical proficiency.

Another aspect of the explanation may be the typical rhetorical context. Because speakers (when not students engaged in "school writing") normally had superior status, there was little need for overt ethical or logical appeals: the context, especially the Confucian relations within both the family and the bureaucratic feudal society, already presumed that listeners had a responsibility to accept and carry out what the speaker urged; the key purpose of the rhetoric was to make certain listeners understood clearly and were moved to act wholeheartedly on that understanding. The speaker's position was thus more like that of Augustine's preacher than of Cicero's advocate.

In more equal relationships, the same rhetorical pattern could be motivated by a need to avoid the crude assertiveness of an overly direct statement. In a conflictive situation, an overly direct statement could lead to a loss of face for one's adversary and therefore fail as a persuasion.

The importance of repetition for the communication of emphasis in Chinese discourse may be yet another aspect of the explanation. In much Chinese discourse the importance of a statement to the speaker is demonstrated by how often the speaker reiterates it, a type of emphasis that often violates the norms of Western professional discourse and frustrates Westerners who do not understand why a point that has already been communicated—or perhaps even "refuted"—is being repeated.

All of these hypotheses are consistent with the Taoist dialectic, which, in the thirteenth century, became part of the neo-Confucian synthesis and thus of mainstream Chinese culture (Needham).

Hessami's brief contrastive study of Iranian and Anglo-Canadian newspaper editorials, although less dramatic than Chinese/English contrasts, also suggests important distinctions. In this sample, a typical Farsi paragraph had five or six levels of generality, in contrast to three or four for the English paragraphs. This did not, however, indicate more detailed development in Farsi; on the contrary, the English editorials had more factual detail. But the Iranian editorials had much more repetition and imagery. This structure manifests itself both through long passages and in single sentences, as in the following instance:

(1) It won't be long before our innocent children, under the gradual effects of this toxic system, will be poisoned culturally, (2) and then we will have a brainwashed, petrified generation, (3) and in other words we will have members of "God's party," who will have no patience to listen to ideas different from their own, who will not hesitate to react violently to other ideas, a quarrelsome generation, drowned in religious ignorance, a superstitious generation who will kill in the name of justice, a generation who will commit suicide in the name of martyrdom, a destructive generation instead of a constructive one.

Conciseness and understatement are apparently not stylistic values in Iranian editorials: quite a different rhetoric seeks quite a different effect.

Aiming at a more subtle cultural distinction, I have collected matrixes drawn for samples of academic sociological writing, some written in English by Anglo-Canadians, some written in French by French-Canadians. My hypothesis is that the influence of Cartesian rationalism may produce more deductive patterns in the French, while the influence of British empiricism may produce more inductive patterns in the English. Some Canadian academics already insist that such differences exist, but the evidence is intuitive and/or anecdotal. If this hypothesis is borne out to any significant degree, it will allow rhetoricians to help academics (graduate students, for example) who move from French to English Canada or vice versa. If the results even hint at cultural differences in ways of thinking about social problems, the implications could be more broadly important, though they would, of course, need to be confirmed by considerable additional research.

To make definitive generalizations, even about Chinese and English discourse, would require considerably more research spread over a much wider range of discourse. The conclusions my colleagues and I have been able to draw are, however, suggestive and tend to match the intuitive insights of those familiar with both cultures. Pending further research, they should be of some value to teachers. More to the point here, they confirm the power of the discourse matrix for investigating such questions.

Poor Writing

Writing is more easily read when

1. the discourse is regular (i.e, patterned),
2. the pattern is familiar to the readers,
3. paragraph indents, transitions, and other cohesion cues accurately signal the semantic pattern, and
4. irrelevant information (unpatterned interruptions, material that falls outside the pattern) is excluded.

Matrix analysis can be used to make apparent and explain flaws in writing. The same flaws can, of course, be explained verbally, but the matrix can make them easier to understand. This is especially true with student writers who are studying composition precisely because their verbal abilities are weak.[21] Consider the following example, produced by a basic writing student at Boston University.

(1) I started reading before I started school. (2) My mother always encouraged my reading. (3) When I was young she would take the time to read to me and also try and teach me to read. (4) I can remember the first volume of *The Nancy Drew Mystery Stories* that my mother bought for me, and my faithfully reading and buying the other volumes until I had completed the set. (5) In the fourth grade, my mother made a big fuss with the principal of my school because my teacher would not let me read if I finished my work early. (6) In the fifth and sixth grades I won first place in the school library contest.

(7) The point that I'm trying to make is that I've been brought up to believe that reading is full of pleasure, not tedious as some people say it is. (8) Reading also expands vocabulary by implementing new words that you can either understand from context or by looking them up in a dictionary. (9) Books expand your knowledge by going into detail and initiating new subject matter.

Although its basic theme, thesis, and structure are valid, this piece of writing has various weaknesses, including considerable imprecision in word choice, which complicates semantic analysis. Nonetheless, we can draw the matrix like this:

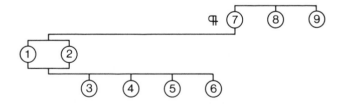

However one analyzes the interrelationships among the first six T-units—sentence 6, for example, although strictly irrelevant as stated, could easily be tied to the general point if it were rephrased slightly—the entire first paragraph clearly supports a generalization actually stated at the beginning of the second paragraph. Sentences 8 and 9, by contrast, totally lack support. Knowing the student and the context, I suppose that she started composing with a general notion of writing about what reading signifies to her, that she realized after drafting sentence 6 that her point was not explicit (and neither was the connection to her assigned purpose, to write about a single signifier which had distinct significations for different people), that she then paused (hence the indent) and added what was missing. After she wrote sentence 7, I imagine her thinking of her audience (an English teacher) and deciding she had better say something more about reading than just that it is pleasurable. Thus she added two additional points parallel to that one. Throughout, like many basic writers, she revised by adding material at the end to modify the total effect, not by going back and changing what was already drafted.

It is always more difficult to talk about *what is missing* than about errors that are present in a piece of writing. In this case, the lack of symmetry in the drawing makes the point with great vividness. The best solution to the structural weakness of this piece would be to add development of sentences 8 and 9, and the matrix virtually suggests that this could easily be done by preceding each of them with sentences parallel to 1–6 and indenting *after* each generalization. Using this kind of inductive development as initiated by the student, one might then want to add a concluding paragraph that would encompass all three general propositions and ultimately assert something like, "To me, reading is good because it signifies pleasure as well as an opportunity to build my vocabulary and expand my knowledge." Or since the matter turns out to comprise one (unstated) main point supported by three subordinate points, one could turn it into a standard five-paragraph essay, as the student might well have done had that form been in her repertoire.

Sometimes matrix analysis, with or without actual diagramming, reveals the potential cognitive coherence of an incoherent text. Take, for example, the following paragraph also written by a basic writer (remembering that T-units encompassing quotations are here treated as equivalent to "So-and-so said, 'X'").

(1) To the poor man (lower class) living in the slums of the city, money signifies the comforts and luxuries he will never know but can only dream

of because he can't even afford the necessities of food, medical care and clothing his family needs. (2) The American population consists of immigrants from many countries. (3) (The American Indian is becoming more and more non-existent.) (4) I asked my grandmother why she came to America, (5) and her response was a common one which I learned in school, "America is the land of opportunity." (6) My French grand-uncle wants his son and daughter to move to America so that they and their children can flourish in the land of plenty. (7) The Irish, Italian, Armenian, Bulgarian, Chinese, Russian, German, Moslem, Hungarian, Japanese, and the most recent example, the Vietnamese (and etc. . . .) flowed and still flow into the dream land of prosperity. (8) Although for the majority America turns out to be a better place to live compared to what they've left behind, the factory worker and unemployed worker can see but only dream of having the boy next door wash his Cadillac.

On first reading, this paragraph certainly seems incoherent: the first two sentences have no apparent connection; although 2–3 and 4–5–6 hang together, there is no clear transition from 3 to 4; despite "the dream land of prosperity," 7 fits better as support for 2 than as a generalization of 4–5–6; and only after 8 does it become really clear what 1 has to do with the overall paragraph.

If we classify T-units according to level of generality and group them, however, we find a generalization, 8, supported by three propositions: (1) almost all Americans are immigrants (2, 3, 7); (2) immigrants come to the United States seeking prosperity (4–5–6); (3) but there is poverty in the United States (1). Together with some sentence-level revision—such as taking 3, which is essentially an afterthought that occurred to the writer upon producing 2, and making it a subordinate clause of 2—this analysis provides the key to a coherent revision. The cognitive basis for the analysis—what the writer needs to learn in order to do the revision himself—is classifying the T-units (or sentences) according to level of generality, thus locating the generalization and subgeneralizations.

This grouping is, of course, similar to the informal clustering activities teachers and writers already use. What the matrix allows is more precision, more structure, and sorting according to level of generality. It also connects this activity to a coherent body of theory.

Pedagogy

Clearly the preceding applications of the discourse matrix suggest various potential uses in teaching composition. Any improved description of discourse structure is, of its nature, a basis for improved instruction. The matrix can be used to describe particular structures for students. It can be used to help them contrast structures they already know with those they need, thus enabling them to use appropriate structures and develop transformation rules to get from familiar to new structures. It can be used to help them see gaps, faulty development, and misorganization in pieces they have drafted. It may even clarify the function of advanced forms of punctuation (see below and appendix C). Many of the pedagogies suggested by Christensen and those who have followed him can be presented in terms of the matrix, perhaps with improved clarity.

Probably most important, used in the context of the New Rhetoric and the Christensen tradition, the matrix provides a set of concepts for unifying various aspects of discourse usually discussed piecemeal and/or as static oppositions: invention and arrangement, form and process, cohesion cues (especially transitions) and semantic structure, organization, style and punctuation, language and thought, reading and writing.

Thinking

One of the most important potential applications of the matrix is in teaching nontraditional students, both those who traditionally did not have access to postsecondary education and those who traditionally did not succeed in humanities courses. Unlike traditional students, these students often lack an intuitive grasp of the basis of modern Western professional/academic discourse—also known as "logic," at least to those ethnocentric enough not to realize this discourse embodies just one particular logic, albeit the one underlying modern science and dominant among modern Western professionals.

These students need to learn the types of thinking, reading, and writing required in modern academic and professional contexts— and that at center is one task. Though it implies certain ways of reading and writing, the most critical aspect of that task is cognitive, for the same logic underlies the structure of academic/professional thinking, reading, and writing. And one major virtue of the matrix is its potential to unify our presentation of that one task by allowing us to talk about the structures and processes of reading, writing, and thinking with one set of concepts and one graphic representation. It should be noted that the concepts underlying discourse matrix analysis can be used without the matrix itself. Kris Gutierrez reports, for example, that the concept of levels of generality allows her basic writing students to comment on each others' writing with assertions like, "Everything here is a level one or level two, you need some level three and four statements to back up what you're saying" (personal communication, 1983). Just having the concept of levels of generality and the notion that English expository paragraphs typically use three or four levels seems to give these basic writers a way to name the problem that makes clear what the solution should be. Similarly, my advanced students use the concept of levels of generality without the matrix to analyze specialized types of discourse they are about to learn.

With composition teachers or with advanced undergraduate writers, I have generally preceded discussion of the matrix with a unit on the cumulative sentence. Christensen's excellent pedagogy for teaching the cumulative sentence introduces such concepts as *level of generality, modification, texture,* and *generative form* (the notion that a rhetorical pattern is not only a way of organizing information, but also a form to be "filled"—hence a generative or heuristic device).[22]

From Christensen's concept of a generative rhetoric, the transition is easy to linking the process of thinking and the structure of discourse which represents and communicates that thinking. One can, for example, use the sorts of activities Mina Shaughnessy suggests, generalization exercises in which the items on a list or chart are presented as the lowest level of generality (data). For, by definition, all the items (except headings) on a list or chart are on one level of generality. The students are led to generalize several times from the list, then to generalize again from their generalizations, and then to make a judgment about this last generalization. They are then shown how to write an essay that contains four levels of generality (data from the list, the first set of generalizations, the encompassing generalization, and the judgment), perhaps with the higher-level generalization as a thesis sentence and the judgment as an ending.[23]

With advanced students the point is to show them that, intuitively, they already understand the basic concept, that there is a relationship between the ways they think and the patterns they are or should be producing in their writing. A simplified version of the matrix can then be presented as visual analogy to make explicit something they intuitively understand.

Writing

Once students grasp the conceptual essence of this sort of discourse analysis, various applications are possible. The matrix or its underlying concepts can be used

1. to help students analyze and revise confused, underdeveloped, or overdeveloped passages in their own writing;
2. to teach students particular patterns they do not yet know;
3. to explain the aspect of readability which has to do neither with sentence structure nor with vocabulary, but which follows from readers' formal expectations (i.e., from their anticipating and/or recognizing patterns of development);
4. to show students how to teach themselves new genres of writing; and
5. to unify, conceptually and in practice, the several departments of rhetoric and various aspects of composition, perhaps even the principles underlying advanced punctuation.

The first application is fairly straightforward, operating in the same way as the "reading is full of pleasure" and "America, land of prosperity" examples (pages 62 and 63–64). The second operates as in Fahey's pedagogy or Jia's: the matrix concepts and drawings become a way of explaining explicitly the pattern to be imitated or avoided. The third allows us to apply a formal principle from the New Rhetoric[24] and modern reading theory to the practical problem of readability, which is too often reduced to its quantifiable aspects (sentence complexity and vocabulary difficulty).

One of the most advanced and most interesting applications of the matrix is based on the assumption that different rhetorical patterns predominate in different types of writing, that an advanced writing student who knows how to write well-developed paragraphs for academic essays may not know the appropriate patterns for other types of writing tasks. Students in my advanced writing classes are, therefore, asked to teach themselves how to do some type of writing that is new and interesting to them. The matrix analysis is, of course, only one part of the overall analysis, which includes questions about the substance, rhetorical context, structure, style, format, and mechanics of the particular type of writing. (See Coe, "A Heuristic," and Brosnahan et al.)

One of the more exciting potentials of a composition pedagogy based on the discourse matrix and the Christensen tradition is the possibility it offers of using certain key terms and basic concepts to discuss various aspects of writing. Not only can these basic concepts be used to clarify the underlying unity of various sorts of structures (sentence structure and discourse structure, style and organization); but they extend even to the level of punctuation, at least insofar as certain hypotheses put forth by Dean Memering and Christensen can be confirmed.

Christensen's basic point is that expert writers generate more information than novice writers do and they add this extra information to their basic statements as modifiers (typically, he argues, creating cumulative sentences). This extra information, he asserts, is most commonly extra detail, on a lower level of generality than the basic statements being modified, and its inclusion creates what he calls *texture*, what makes us describe a piece of writing as being "well developed" or as having "depth." Christensen wants us to teach sentence patterns not as sentence-combining exercises (in which students create more complex syntax by combining in one sentence information originally contained in several sentences), but as generative forms that will encourage students to invent more information, more specifics, which they will use to develop more texture, more depth, in their writing. Thus a dialectic is established between arrangement and invention.

As Shaughnessy emphasizes, experienced writers have the ability to stick with and elaborate on a point long after basic writers have moved on to the next point. Pedagogies such as those of Rebekah Caplan (described in Caplan and Keech, esp. 109–12) and Fahey (described above) demonstrate that formal structures can be used to help basic writers understand both what is expected of them and how to provide that development. Matrix analysis helps advanced students realize where and how they can add texture, further developing not just sentences, but also paragraphs and longer passages.

Memering's hypothesis about relations of generality across colons, semicolons, and formal dashes is essentially an insightful rewriting of seven rules commonly found in handbooks. It unites under one principle four colon rules, two semicolon rules, and one dash rule—and allows a terminological shift from "rules" (with the connotation of being hard-and-fast) to "guiding principle" (with the connotation of being generally true) as well as a shift to the notion of punctuation as a cue one provides for readers, not something one does to texts (personal communication, 1974). In short, this hypothesis is that what follows a colon is subordinate to what precedes it, that what follows a semicolon is coordinate with what precedes it, and that what follows a formal dash is superordinate to what precedes it. Christensen's hypothesis about "paragraph punctuation"—that what makes two independent clauses so "closely related" they should be in one sentence is not intrinsic to the two clauses but must be understood in terms of their function relative to the rest of the passage—is even more interesting and may provide a basis for explaining something that previously could only be modeled. (See appendix C.)

Reading

The matrix provides an instrument for teaching students how to abstract the gist or macrostructure of a text and how to grasp the relationship between that gist and the other parts of the text. The matrix, therefore, seems inherently suitable for applying pedagogically the insights of psycholinguists about how readers re-create meaning. Zhu Wei-fang's use of matrix analysis in teaching intensive reading to first-year students of English at the Beijing Foreign Language Institute indicates some of this potential ("Discourse Analysis in Language Teaching").

Intensive reading, probably the most common course in foreign language curricula in China, is quite different from reading courses in the West. Irene Brosnahan has argued convincingly that it is really language study, much more intensive than anything anyone would normally do while reading. For reasons related to how reading is taught in China (which, in turn, reflects the basically morphemic nature of the Chinese language) and to the dominance of grammar-translation as a method of teaching foreign languages, intensive reading includes studying the vocabulary of a passage (pronunciation, spelling, inflectional and derivational forms, exact meaning and usage), studying the grammar of each sentence (parts of speech, grammatical functions, sentence patterns, exact and correct usage), recitation, memorization, and translation.

> Intensive reading is essentially very intensive language study, reminiscent of the study of Chinese classics. The reading passages are often very difficult, with a lot of new vocabulary items and complex grammatical structures, and often on topics that are esoteric or heavily culture-bound. (I recall being asked to explain and translate a passage on Roosevelt at Yalta by one of the young women working in our residence in Shanghai who could hardly understand the simple English exchanges of the dining room. She was preparing for a test in her intensive reading class.) The instruction in intensive reading is necessarily a laborious word-by-word, phrase-by-phrase, sentence-by-sentence explanation through translation. The sentences are parsed and analyzed carefully to obtain the exact meaning in Chinese. Questions and discussion of usage are often very picky and sometimes trivial. There are usually two main preoccupations in this mental exercise: (1) when there is a difference in surface form between two similar expressions, which is correct, or what is the exact difference in meaning or usage between the two? and (2) how does one translate any expression in English *exactly* into Chinese and vice versa?

Brosnahan distinguished five levels of reading: language study, study-reading, general fluent reading, skimming, and scanning. She then argued that Chinese intensive reading courses are really language *study* (analysis of the language), not reading (i.e., not practice using the language). What the Chinese call extensive reading she compared with what Western students do when studying for an exam ("careful reading of text for full understanding and recall of main ideas and details"), though she asserted that in practice it differs from intensive reading "only in degree rather than in kind."

In teaching her intensive reading class, Zhu would ordinarily have spent four hours on a typical short excerpt of perhaps twenty sentences: two hours of explanation and question-and-answer, an hour of exercises, and an hour of retelling. Experimentally, she used only twenty minutes for explanation and then presented a conceptual diagram of the text based on her matrix analysis. Without the usual questions/answers or exercises (but with the usual considerable time for preparation), all her students were able to retell the text without looking at the diagram or the text; more important, their retelling was no longer recitation of memorized words but genuine retelling based on memory of meaning, reorganized as points supporting a thesis—memory, that is, of the gist.

To verify her subjective impression that the new pedagogy was more effective than the standard one she had been using, Zhu repeated her experiment, this time using cloze pretests and posttests to measure comprehension. In evaluating the cloze tests, she distinguished between semantic and syntactic gaps.

Stuff a _____ handkerchief into the bottom _____ a glass so that it will not _____ out when the glass is turned _____ down.

The first gap is semantic, and the missing information is available two sentences later when the text says "[something] will still be dry." The second gap is syntactic in the sense that the syntax of the sentence makes clear what word is missing. On a pretest, only eight of twenty-three students filled the first blank correctly; all twenty-three supplied the missing *of* for the second blank. The discourse matrix pedagogy, probably because it shifted students' attention from words and surface structure to meaning, reduced such semantic errors by an average of 32 percent.

Although one can hardly draw conclusions from such a limited pilot study, Zhu's results are suggestive, in part because they are consistent both with the general theory of a cognitive/communicative approach to second language learning and with New Rhetorical theory. Zhu hypothesizes that the discourse matrix pedagogy helps students to see the underlying logic of the text, to comprehend more intelligently, to read with anticipation, and to be more sensitive to contextual cues in the sentences surrounding the one they are reading. One might further hypothesize that the development of such reading abilities would enable students to revise their drafts better when writing.

While it is certainly premature to make major claims for pedagogies based on the discourse matrix, it does not seem premature to assert that the limited evidence is sufficiently consistent with New Rhetorical theories of composition—and with our intuitions as experienced teachers of writing—to indicate that the matrix has pedagogical potential worth exploring. I hope what has been presented here constitutes an attractive invitation that will induce others to join in that exploration.

5

Implications

[I]n *failing* to define a form, one may *actually* fall into critical errors.

—Kenneth Burke (*Language* 42)

What was altered in the seventeenth century . . . was the way in which one wrote down what one observed and, by means of a series of statements, recreated a perceptual process; it was the relation and interplay of subordinations . . . the reciprocal positions of particular observations and general principles. Natural History . . . above all . . . [became] a set of rules for arranging statements in series, an obligatory set of schemata of dependence, of order, and of successions, in which the recurrent elements that may have value as concepts were distributed.

—Michel Foucault (57)

THE THEORY AND RESEARCH PRESENTED HERE DOES NOT ALLOW very firm conclusions about particulars. Though it indicates some directions for more effective teaching of form and structure, the validity of those directions needs to be confirmed by further research as well as by the experiences of both writers and writing teachers. My research collaborators and I have perhaps made some contribution to the understanding of paragraphing and of certain distinctions between Chinese and English discourse structures. I would like to believe we have suggested how concepts from the Christensen tradition and the New Rhetoric have the potential to unify disparate aspects of composition theory and pedagogy. Primarily I trust we have successfully introduced the discourse matrix as a useful instrument and significant step toward a "grammar of passages."

Problems assuredly remain. Like any representational system, the discourse matrix will best be perfected through use. It is, moreover, only one component of a text "grammar"; it deals with discourse in the sense that it looks "beyond the sentence" at the structure of passages. Regarding the other crucial sense of the term *discourse*, the relationship between texts and their communicative contexts, the discourse matrix can only raise and focus our questions; for it delineates contextual relationships of statements only within the text (except insofar as other contexts are implicit in the act of reading).

To explain the structures discovered by the matrix, however, we must move to this next level of analysis, to the relationships with communicative contexts. The discourse matrix does raise well-defined questions that lead toward contextual explanations, such as our attempts in chapter 4 (pages 59–60) to provide rationales for the distinctions between Chinese and English discourse. Although our level of analysis is quite different from his, the matrix brings us to the kinds of interrelationships that concern Foucault, especially the relationship between statements and the contexts defined by what Foucault calls enunciative modalities: "the statement, as it emerges in its materiality, appears with a status, enters various networks and various fields of use, is subjected to transferences or modifications, is integrated into operations and strategies in which its identity is maintained or effaced" (105)—the statement, in short, as rhetorical. This is a context broader than those normally considered by pragmatic linguists or psychologists, but more limited than those normally considered by economic or environmental determinists and more specifically historical and material than those normally considered by historians of ideas. It is a context of power, of effects.

Foucault's "first question" is: "[W]ho is speaking? Who . . . is accorded the right," who is "qualified" to "use this sort of language [*langage*]?" (50). Our first question should be: What are the relationships between formal structures "in" the text and "enunciative" contexts? To what extent, for instance, does the ability to use certain conventional forms "accord the right" to make certain types of statements? To what extent does restricting knowledge of appropriate forms, if only by leaving it tacit, silence classes of people? To answer such questions, we must be able to describe the structure of state-ments—not of sentences, not of propositions, but of statements—represented in the text, and the discourse matrix is a step toward such description. This particular set of questions requires us some-times to work from language to function. Though discourse matrix analysis seems to violate Foucault in its operational assumption of correspondence between a grammatically defined unit of language (T-unit, clause, or sentence) and a unit of meaning-in-context (state-ment), it is actually consistent with Foucault's more general prin-ciple of allowing the problem to define the relevant evidence and his assertion that the function which distributes signs (i.e., the state-ment) is manifest in language.

Karen LeFevre argues that to understand rhetorical invention we must consider it as a social act. Surely rhetorical form is equally, if not more, social. And surely one way invention becomes social is when an individual's act of invention is mediated by conventional forms preferred or prescribed by a discourse community. One way discourse communities preserve their boundaries, their integrity, is by restricting the communications of those who have not learned the conventional forms—and the most important of these conven-tional forms often are not those described in handbooks and "style" manuals, but those which govern the structure, interrelationships, and validation of statements.

James Berlin argues that "rhetoric is always at the center of the educational enterprise" because

> Rhetoric teachers are entrusted with the responsibility of passing on to young people a given society's sanctioned rules governing reading, writ-ing, and speaking. The main business of rhetoric teachers is in fact to in-culcate these rules and to determine who has learned them and who has not. The rules themselves are usually tacit—are usually beyond the realm of discussion, falling in the realm of epistemology. . . . In teaching writing and speaking, we are providing our students with instructions for the correct experiencing of reality, offering implicit directives for what ought and ought not to be experienced and communicated. "Rhetoric and Literacy" (257–66)

Frances Christie adds that "those who fail in schools are those who fail to master the genres of schooling: the ways of structuring and dealing with experience which schools value in varying degrees"

(24). We might extend that statement to other academic and professional communities, defining certain types of form as an aspect of the "disciplinary matrix" with which Thomas Kuhn explains the unity of such communities (182).

The discourse matrix matters in part because it approaches formal values that lie on the boundary between what composition teachers label "coherence" and what they label "logic" on the margins of student papers. It may also matter because it approaches values Richard Ohmann says composition teachers deflect when they advise students to "use definite, specific, concrete language" (390). One of the potentials of literacy is the opening up of what Burke titles "the dialectic of transcendence":

> a mode of interpretation [that treats] empirical things-here-and-now *in terms of a Beyond* (be this, in its simplest form, but a way to view terms of lower generalization as inspirited by terms of higher generalization). Obviously such a dialectic has notable rhetorical implications since the view of things *hic et nunc* in terms of a Beyond implies a corresponding attitude towards them, with corresponding implications of policy or action. (*Language* 299; cf. appendix A)

Not so much for what it will show in and of itself, but for how it can be used in answering broader questions, the creation of a "grammar of passages" is one of the more urgent projects facing composition theorists and researchers, rhetoricians, and teachers of writing. Without such a "grammar," various important questions in these disciplines cannot be properly answered and various significant goals cannot be achieved. In the context of that need, this book has attempted a step toward a "grammar of passages," seeking to demonstrate

1. that the Christensen tradition contains powerful concepts which can be used to create at least part of such a "grammar,"
2. that the discourse matrix is a useful instrument for implementing the concepts of Christensen and others,
3. that the discourse matrix has significant potential for various pressing tasks—among them the description of standard discourse structures, analysis of specialized discourses, contrastive rhetoric, explanation of certain types of punctuation, explanation of "bad" writing—and, consequently has significant potential for composition pedagogy, and

4. that a potential exists to unify composition theory in such a way as to make more coherent the complex of rules, principles, and processes faced by novice writers.

If beyond these potentials some of the specifics asserted on the basis of preliminary studies are somewhat accurate and useful, so much the better. For "this study is theoretical only that it may become practical" (Richards 19).

Appendix A
Generalization and Abstraction

Richard Coe, Wendy Watson, and Susan Fahey

AS NOTED ABOVE, THE TERM *ABSTRACT* IS USED IN DISCUSSIONS OF composition theory and pedagogy to refer to four distinguishable processes:

1. generalizing (as in inductive reasoning),
2. abstracting as it occurs preconsciously in human perception,
3. abstracting as it functions in concept formation and deductive thinking,
4. communicating with abstract (rather than concrete) diction.

Generalization, Ann Berthoff emphasizes, "is what rhetoric chiefly describes: generalization is at the heart of all discourse and of course it is central to concept formation. But it is not the only mode of abstraction" ("Intelligent Eye" 196). That is to say, there is a process through which we reach, for example, the concept *flower* by generalizing from roses, daisies, etc.; Susanne Langer calls this "generalizing abstraction" (*Mind* 153).[25] Although this is not the only type of abstraction, it predominates in our empirical scientific culture to the point that we often carelessly take it as the only process of concept formation. Indeed, Berthoff argues that

one of the chief reasons composition theory is stymied is the dependence upon a brass instrument manufactured by General Semantics, the Ladder of Abstraction. Rhetoricians continually use it to explain how we climb from the positive earth to the dangerous ether of concept. But it's that metaphoric ladder itself that's dangerous. We could rename it The Ladder of Degrees of Generality to avoid the misleading notion that all abstraction proceeds by means of generalizing. . . . ("Intelligent Eye" 196)

For the analysis of discursive discourse, generalization is what matters most, and we can solve the immediate problem by calling it *generalization* (and by referring to levels of generality). We can then reserve the term *abstraction* for the cognitive process by which one separates (abstracts) an idea from the object or event that concretely embodies it. C. S. Peirce gives this example:

When we see the little bottle of green crystals, the green idea detaches itself from the remaining ideas, . . . and leads to a thought (which is accurately expressed by the sentence "These crystals are green.") where the green stands off from the remaining ideas. . . . (Rpt. in Berthoff, *Reclaiming the Imagination* 39)

Although both *greenness* and *flower* may be termed abstract, there is an important distinction here. We may emphasize that distinction by saying we *abstracted* the concept of greenness from one or more concrete green objects, but we *generalized* the concept of flower from various specific flowers.

Although the process by which we reach a given concept may involve a combination of generalization and abstraction, it is important to distinguish the two processes, if only so that we remember concept formation involves more than generalizing. Those terms we think of as epitomizing abstraction, such as Love, cannot be reached by simple generalization. Though we may generalize from various *loving acts*, we must abstract the "loving" aspect of the concrete act before we generalize. Abstraction, therefore, inevitably involves deductive as well as inductive process, for only deductive reasoning can guide our selection of what to abstract. Updating an example from L. S. Vygotsky which makes the same point, let us allow that perhaps one can reach the concept *sister* primarily by generalizing from various people's sisters; but the concept of *sisterhood* must be abstracted.

There is, of course, a sense in which perceiving an object as green and discussing sisterhood involve distinct types of abstraction. Indeed, as used by rhetorical theorists from I. A. Richards to Berthoff, the term *abstract* refers to two analogous but qualitatively distinct cognitive processes: preconscious perception and conscious interpretation. Richards and Berthoff, of course, want to emphasize the important sense in which the two processes are similar, the sense in which all human perception is intrinsically an abstraction from reality. For human beings do not see simply: we *see as* and *see that*. To see *that* this is a piece of paper, to see this *as* paper, one preconsciously synthesizes a mass of sensory input with an abstract schema (for paper). Thus, by preconsciously abstracting, human minds reduce the thousands of bits of input that reach our sense organs to patterns, figures, outlines. Thus our perceptions are not "raw data" but representations; we re-present "reality" to ourselves. Our very perceptions are in this sense abstracted from reality.[26]

When Vygotsky describes how children learn to use abstract concepts such as *exploitation* or *brotherhood* to interpret their perceptions, he is still discussing abstraction, but in a qualitatively and logically distinct sense—and abstraction in this sense is more important to educational processes. When people deepen their understandings of their own experiences by juxtaposing those experiences with abstract ideas that (1) highlight certain aspects of the experience and (2) bring to light interrelations which might otherwise be overlooked, they are abstracting in a way qualitatively distinct from the preconscious abstracting that occurs when they first perceive the event. This kind of abstraction—the ability not just to attach the proper abstract label to an event, but also to use an abstraction to generate a fuller and better understanding of the event—is one of the most important intellectual processes learned in schools (Vygotsky chap. 6).[27]

In traditional rhetorical terms, this kind of abstraction has more to do with definition and deductive reasoning (and hence with the Socratic dialectic, which turns on definition) than with generalization or inductive reasoning. While we should understand the sense in which thinking with abstractions is comparable to what people do preconsciously when they perceive, we should not conflate these two types of abstraction.

The stylistic value often denoted "Abst" in red ink on the margins of students' papers derives not from generalization but from the concept of abstraction as in *greenness, love, sisterhood,* and so on. This "abstract" is rhetorical: it refers not so much to the concept represented by a word or phrase as to the effect that word or phrase will have on readers (and broadly, to the sense in which the words are convincing). We call "concrete" the sorts of words and phrases that create vividness in readers' minds; such language usually evokes objects or events that we could experience with our five senses and does so in a way that we metaphorically term "tangible." Abstract words and phrases lack this effect; they are effectively used by writers who want to avoid "impact" and also, when the abstract term happens to be more specific, by writers who want to be precise. This distinction allows us to explain and sometimes validate specialists' preference for certain abstractions, which are more precise than the concrete equivalents. Together with the distinction between perceptual and conceptual abstraction, it also allows us to understand, more generally, how this stylistic value reflects and reproduces the empiricist ideology of our scientific era: as one of the conditions that constrains the dispersion of statements in dominant modern English discourse formations, this declared desire to rid writing of abstraction encourages communication of observations and inductive generalizations; it discourages discourse characterized by a dialectic in which abstract terms serve explicitly as theoretical principles to inform and guide thinking (cf. Ohmann, "Use Definite, Specific, Concrete Language"; cf. Foucault, though this is a sort of enunciative modality he does not discuss).

Appendix B
Other Instruments

The Nold and Davis Matrix

THE DISCOURSE MATRIX PRESENTED IN THIS BOOK IS BASED ON A
matrix previously devised by Nold and Davis. I have modified the
Nold and Davis matrix in two ways. I have replaced the three-
dimensional complexity of the Nold and Davis matrix with a two-
dimensional version that can readily be sketched on paper. At the
same time, I have added descriptive power by using the lines of the
matrix to indicate logical relations. The lines in Nold and Davis' diagrams are redundant: they indicate sequence, which is already indicated by both the numbers and the placement of the circles. Using
the lines to indicate "deep" rather than "surface" structure relationships avoids the need for a three-dimensional diagram, one of the
main obstacles to easy use of Nold and Davis' matrix. (See the first
two figures below for a comparison of the Nold and Davis matrix and
the revised matrix.)

The three-dimensional complexity of Nold and Davis' matrix
allows them to make one important distinction: by using the third
dimension, they distinguish a T-unit that reiterates a point made
previously (restatement) from one that introduces a new subtopic.
This is, of course, an important distinction (one, incidentally, that
allows Nold and Davis to define node strings as horizontal lines
within a plane). A new stadium, and thus a potential paragraph indentation, occurs when a new subtopic is introduced, but not when
a short passage ends with a regeneralization that repeats its topic
sentence.

Essentially, Nold and Davis distinguish two types of coordination. One kind restates a point already made (and thus is "in the same plane"); the other kind introduces a new subtopic ("new plane"). The second type creates what Rodgers would call a new stadium; the first does not. Nold and Davis' assertion that superordination may move up *or back to another plane* serves to make this same distinction.

However, this one distinction, which is actually made by comparing the T-unit in question with the previous passage (not just with the previous T-unit, as Nold and Davis' instructions suggest it should be), is a high price to pay for the three-dimensional complexity of the matrix. What I have done, therefore, is to devise a way to use the lines of the matrix to make this same distinction. The figures shown below represent the Nold and Davis matrix and the revised matrix as they would be drawn for Nold and Davis' reading of the sample paragraph on page 39. In this paragraph, according to Nold and Davis' analysis, T-units *1, 2, 11, 12,* and *14* are all on the same level of generality. But, they assert, only *2, 11,* and *14* constitute a

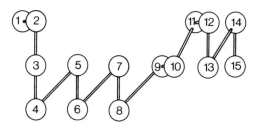

Nold and Davis reading, original matrix

node string. Their analysis is correct: the passage does make only three points, not five. The opening T-unit, through contrast, sets up the writer's first real point (2).

Note that Nold and Davis indicate repetition on the same level of generality, *1–2, 11–12,* by changing planes. It is important that the matrix drawing show clearly that the passage has three points, that *11* and *12* represent the same point. But by using the revised matrix, we can distinguish repetition on the same level of generality from other types of coordination simply by the way we draw the connecting lines. Thus we eliminate the need for a three-dimensional diagram.

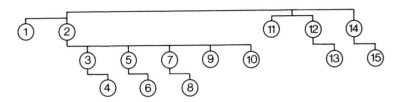

Nold and Davis reading, revised matrix

For ease of contrast, I have reproduced here a two-dimensional matrix drawing based on Nold and Davis' reading; as explained in chapter 3, however, the passage contains two ambiguous relationships. First, Nold and Davis read the opening two T-units as coordinate, as contrasting two types of amazement. However, these two T-units can also be read as statements about amazement in general and the amazement provoked by *War and Peace* in particular, in which case the second is subordinate to the first. Nold and Davis' reading is certainly possible, but the second reading is probably better. In fact, Nold and Davis vacillated before settling on their reading (Nold, personal communication, 1981).

Second, and similarly, the tenth T-unit can (and probably should) be read as a more specific explanation of the ninth, as explaining more specifically what it means to "look at the thing itself" (i.e., *10* may be read as having roughly the same relationship to 9 that 8 has to 7, 6 to 5, and 4 to 3). Nold and Davis' reading was apparently influenced by a shifting cohesion cue: the semicolons that connect 3 to 4, 5 to 6, and 7 to 8 are succeeded by a period between 9 and 10. I take this, however, as another kind of emphasis, as an indication that *9–10* is not just another item on the list but rather the most important item, to which the list has been building. My reading would be diagrammed as in the following figure.

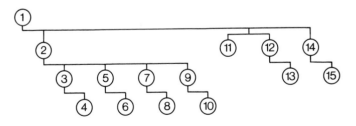

Coe reading

Although the implications are less significant, I think it is also possible to suggest readings other than Nold and Davis' by asking the following questions: does *9* encompass *3, 5,* and *7*? is *11* coordinate or subordinate to *2*? is *14* superordinate to *12*? That is, we need to decide the level of a T-unit relative not only to the preceding T-unit, but also relative to the rest of the discourse. Although the relative level of, say, *13* and *7/8* is difficult to establish, it is also not psycholinguistically relevant. But the relative levels of *2, 11, 12,* and *14* do matter—which means we must sometimes ask not just whether a T-unit is subordinate or superordinate, but also *how* subordinate, *how* superordinate it is.

Topical Structure Analysis

Witte's instrument for diagramming topical structure[28] is in some ways comparable to the discourse matrix. If the grammatical subjects of the independent clauses in a passage were also always the logical subjects of the propositions those clauses communicate, and if the subject of a proposition could always be taken to stand for the whole proposition, then topical structure analysis would produce the same results as discourse matrix analysis. But these assumptions do not always hold.

The distinction between topical structure analysis and discourse matrix analysis is readily apparent when we contrast Witte's figure illustrating topical structure analysis of the following passage with a matrix diagram of the same passage.

. . . (6) *Fantasies* differ according to what people deem as their most important goals in life. (7) A *small businessman*, for example, may see himself crushing giant corporations as his own business gets started and as he hopes for future success. (8) An *intern* in medical school may see himself developing a new surgical procedure that will one day save millions of lives. (9) A beginning *college freshman* may fantasize that he will graduate with honors and be offered the best job in his graduating class.

(10) *My own fantasies*, like those of others, are shaped by what I want my life to be when I finish college. (11) Sometimes, *I* fantasize that I am Terry Bradshaw leading the Steelers to another Super Bowl championship. (12) At other times, *I* dream that I will someday own my own fleet of

shrimp boats or be able to ski like Phil Mahre. (13) But whenever *I* fantasize, I know I am escaping the reality of being a freshman at the University of Texas. . . .

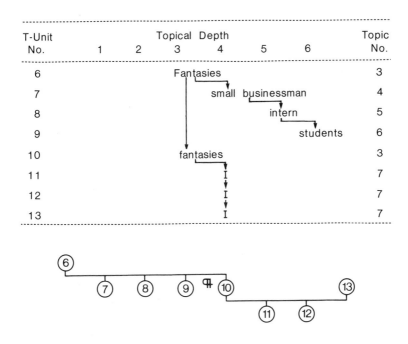

Note that the second paragraph of this excerpt does not really initiate a new topic but continues the topic of the first, that sentence *10* is distinguished only by the shift from "businessman-intern-college freshman" to "I" as exemplification of the proposition stated in sentence *6* (and the "I" is a college freshman). Although one could argue about whether *10* is really quite on the same level as 7-8-9, it is clearly subordinate to *6*. What seems to happen, cognitively, in the student's writing process is that the detailed development of the proposition stated in sentence *6* ultimately leads to specific personal examples that contradict (or at least indicate the inadequacy of) that proposition, leading the student to introduce a new proposition (*13*) that helps to explain the examples more fully—and this new subtopic is introduced without being cued by a paragraph indent. True, this is student writing, but consider an interesting paragraph written by Bertrand Russell which uses a similar structure, developing two major propositions that are linked in mid-paragraph by a common example. (This, the first paragraph of an essay entitled "How to Grow Old," is a keyhole paragraph—but not the type described by Sheridan Baker (62–63) and other traditional textbook writers.)

> In spite of the title, this article will really be on how not to grow old, which, at my time of life, is a much more important subject. My first advice would be to choose your ancestors carefully. Although both my parents died young, I have done well in this respect as regards my other ancestors. My maternal grandfather, it is true, was cut off in the flower of his youth, at the age of sixty-seven, but my other three grandparents all lived to be over eighty. Of remoter ancestors I can only discover one who did not live to a great age, and he died of a disease which is now rare, namely, having his head cut off. A great-grandmother of mine, who was a friend of Gibbon, lived to the age of ninety-two, and to her last day remained a terror to all her descendants. My maternal grandmother, after having nine children who survived, one who died in infancy, and many miscarriages, as soon as she became a widow devoted herself to women's higher education. She was one of the founders of Girton College, and worked hard at opening the medical profession to women. She used to relate how she met in Italy an elderly gentleman who was looking very sad. She inquired the cause of his melancholy and he said that he had just parted from his two grandchildren. "Good gracious," she exclaimed, "I have seventy-two grandchildren, and if I were sad each time I parted from one of them, I should have a dismal existence!" "Madre snaturale," he replied. But speaking as one of the seventy-two, I prefer her recipe. After the age of eighty she found she had some difficulty in getting to sleep, so she habitually spent the hours from midnight to 3 a.m. in reading popular science. I do not believe that she ever had time to notice that she was growing old. This, I think, is the proper recipe for remaining young. If you have wide and keen interests and activities in which you can still be effective, you will have no reason to think about the merely statistical fact of the number of years you have already lived, still less of the probable brevity of your future. (Rpt. in Wu et al. 11–12)

Russell's first topic sentence is, "My first advice [about how *not* to grow old] would be to choose [long-lived] ancestors." His second advice, in the same paragraph, about how *not* to grow old is to "have wide and keen interests and activities in which you can still be effective, [so] you will have no reason to think about . . . the probable brevity of your future." At mid-paragraph, Russell neatly uses the coincidence that his maternal grandmother exemplifies both propositions to slip unnoticed from one point to the next. Shall we say that Russell here wrote a "bad" paragraph, or is there more to say about keyhole paragraphs than yet is found in composition textbooks?

Appendix C
Further Hypotheses

Paragraphing

A SHIFT OF PERSPECTIVE AND CONSIDERABLE RESEARCH IS NEEDED to explain the parameters within which competent writers of English prose make their paragraphing decisions. We must stop asking what a paragraph is and start asking what paragraphing (i.e., the initiation of a new paragraph) signals to readers; we must think of paragraphing as a kind of macro-punctuation mark that guides readers' interpretation of passages much as commas guide readers' interpretation of sentences. Then the question seems to divide in two: (1) Where do writers have the option of paragraphing? (2) How do they decide when to exercise such options? I suggest the following hypotheses: New paragraphs may be used to signal

1. the beginning of a stadium,
2. the beginning of a passage that has a distinct rhetorical function (e.g., a transition at least two sentences long, an introduction, a conclusion), and
3. a point where a writer wants to create emphasis by violating the ordinary norms of paragraphing.

This third paragraphing option is comparable to the informal dash used within a sentence for emphasis at a point where there would ordinarily be no punctuation at all; it can be used only very occasionally or it ceases to create the desired emphasis. (Note that all three of these options are defined by writers' communicative purposes.)

If these options sufficiently explain where paragraphs may begin in most kinds of modern English prose, let me suggest three hypothetical factors that may explain writers' decisions to indent or not indent at these points:

1. a rule of thumb which suggests that modern readers of English perceive a paragraph as "dense" and "difficult" once its format on the page becomes much longer than it is wide (i.e., a piece composed of shorter paragraphs tends to appear more "readable" while one composed of longer paragraphs tends to appear more "sophisticated," in part because longer paragraphs often do interrelate more topics),
2. the occasion, i.e., genre and communicative situation (see the section "Specialized Discourses," page 48ff), and
3. the "stylistic" preferences of individual writers.

Thus I hypothesize a multilevel hierarchy of constraints within which competent writers seem to make their paragraphing decisions. That is to say, the extent to which writers exercise the paragraphing options defined by the first three factors depends both on their responses to audience and occasion and, within those parameters, on their individual predilections. Cf., for example, the passage analyzed by Nold and Davis (page 39 above) where an option clearly exists to indent after the tenth T-unit; cf. also the Russell paragraph on page 88.

Punctuation

Dean Memering suggested the relationship between the Christensen tradition and punctuation when he asserted that the proper use of the colon, semicolon, and what I will call the formal dash could be explained in terms of levels of generality.[29] Nonetheless, I did not expect the discourse matrix to yield insights into punctuation practices until, in the process of doing other analyses, I stumbled upon certain apparent patterns. These insights are, however, as yet unconfirmed by any controlled study. I present them here only as tentative hypotheses and only because they indicate another potential use of the discourse matrix.

It is important to remember, of course, that the use of punctuation marks has changed significantly since the middle of the last century, that their use varies considerably in distinct discourses within modern English, and that even published writers often do not use them according to anybody's rules. The function of punctuation is metacommunicative: punctuation tells readers how to read; specifically, it tells them how to perceive sentence structure. Although there is a standard code for English punctuation, I hypothesize that the code is only a guide, that it may be overridden by leaving out punctuation when the structure is clear or by using nonstandard punctuation when that will better serve the function of cueing readers to the structure. Consequently, one can easily find counterexamples to contradict any assertions about how punctuation marks are used. Nonetheless, it is possible to explain the underlying principles that usually govern their use and from which most other usage is a variation.

As a rule, what follows a colon is a more specific equivalent of what preceded it. What follows a formal dash is a more general equivalent of what preceded it. And the clauses on either side of a semicolon are on the same level of generality. This means, among other things, that a sentence with a colon used to punctuate a lead-in can often be reversed to create a distinct emphasis if one substitutes a dash for the colon, thus turning a lead-in into a summation.

These were the courses I took last quarter: English, psychology, history, and philosophy.

English, psychology, history, and philosophy—these were the courses I took last quarter.

After displaying the product and extolling its virtues, he asks the homemaker for a small rug that needs cleaning—that is how his approach works.

His approach works like this: after displaying the product and extolling its virtues, he asks the homemaker for a small rug that needs cleaning.

The reaction of the crowd signified only one thing: apathy.

Apathy—that was the only thing signified by the reaction of the crowd.

These examples and the terms "colon for lead-in," "dash for summation" are derived from Edward P. J. Corbett's *The Little English Handbook* (124–28).

But what is most interesting about the application of concepts from the Christensen tradition to the analysis of punctuation is the insight the discourse matrix seems to offer into writers' decisions to punctuate two independent clauses, which could, of course, have been two sentences, with a semicolon (or a comma plus coordinating conjunction). Traditionally, such decisions have been explained by asserting that the two independent clauses were "so closely related" they should be conjoined in the same sentence. Except to those who already understood the tacit principle intuitively, this never was much of an explanation. Presumably any two consecutive sentences are fairly closely related. Explanations based on parallelism or antithesis are better, but they cover relatively few cases.

There is certainly ground to suspect—though, pending further investigation, this can be asserted only as a hypothesis—that often what makes the two clauses so closely related is that they serve a discourse function parallel to single sentences that precede or follow. Christensen calls this "paragraph punctuation," which he says "usually involves the choice of whether to make compound sentences or not"; he offers the following example:

> The order [of science] is what we find to work, conveniently and instructively. It is not something we stipulate; it is not something we can dogmatise about. It is what we find; it is what we find useful.

The author, says Christensen, "wisely grouped five coordinate statements into three sentences, sorting them out on the basis of content," making clear to readers that the five statements make three points ("Paragraph" 151, 155). Consider, similarly, Bergen Evans' decision to create this compound sentence (in the example on page 35 above).

> Lincoln's vocabulary and his way of pronouncing certain words were sneered at by many better educated people at the time, but he seemed to be able to use the English language as effectively as his critics.

This compound sentence offers an example functionally parallel to the examples offered by the two preceding sentences, neither of which has more than one independent clause. A compound sentence here helps readers realize that, despite the presence of two independent clauses, only one more example is being presented. There being many reasons for compounding sentences with a comma and coordinating conjunction, however, the decision to use a semicolon instead of a period and capital letter is better grist for our mill. Consider, for instance, the use of semicolons in the passage analyzed by Nold and Davis (page 39). The writer clearly uses semicolons to confine each characteristic of childlike amazement to one sentence; replace the semicolons with periods and capital letters, and readers will have more difficulty reading because the verbal cues (*that, such, such*) indicating where the naming of a new characteristic begins are no longer reinforced by punctuation cues.

(1) There is an amazement proper to the experience of all great art, (2) but the special amazement which *War and Peace* revives in me while I am reading it is like that of a child. (3) The child does not expect the unexpected. (4) That would already be a preparation against it. (5) He does not for an instant doubt that a certain event had to happen. (6) Such a doubt obscures. (7) He may even have been told beforehand that it was going to happen. (8) Such foreknowledge is as little a part of him as a label in his cap. (9) He is able to look at the thing itself. (10) The event reaches him radiant with magical causes but not yet trapped in sufficient cause.

The writer of the original version does break the pattern, probably for emphasis, between T-units 9 and 10. The writer also uses a semicolon in just this way between T-units 12 and 13, which make only one point, and uses a comma plus coordinating conjunction to the same end between T-units 14 and 15. Although by the principles hypothesized here colons would seem to be better punctuation (because the second T-unit is always more specific), the function being served (to indicate "very closely related") is normally a semicolon function, and the writer is consistent throughout the passage.

Appendix D
Practice Passage

The following passage, written for another purpose, has a clear enough structure to be a convenient exercise in discourse matrix analysis:

> The discourse matrix is a technique for analyzing and diagramming the structure of meaning represented in a text. What we describe here is a revised and simplified version of the matrix proposed by Nold and Davis, which was based on concepts originated by Christensen and Rodgers. It produces much more detailed analysis of discourse structure than did traditional discussion of paragraph development (in terms of topic sentences, and so forth), but it is simple enough to be used by teachers preparing courses or curricula.
>
> The discourse matrix is somewhat like a "grammar of passages," describing what we consider the most significant aspect of relationships among sentences. Its basic unit is the T-unit. The T-unit (terminable unit) is a string of words that could be punctuated as a sentence. Thus, except in the case of compound sentences, which contain two or more completed stated propositions and thus could be punctuated as two or more sentences, the T-unit is ordinarily the same as the sentence. Psycholinguistically, we presume the T-unit ordinarily represents a single semantic proposition to be transferred from short-term to long-term memory.

Notes

1. Since it is assumed that any item which modifies another must be of a lower level of generality, level of generality and pattern of modification are actually presumed to be two facets of one function. For a review of the literature, see the section titled "The Christensen Tradition" in chapter 2; for a bibliography, see the starred items in the Works Cited.
2. Cf. Erving Goffman's notion of "primary frames" (21–39) and Robin Bell Markels' discussion of "Inferences, Frames and Cohesion" (*New Perspective* 31–33). Kenneth Burke, of course, had made various comparable analyses earlier, although without using the same terminology. See also van Dijk and Kintsch, and Kintsch and van Dijk.

   Cf. Robert de Beaugrande's notion of "frame defense." De Beaugrande argues that a text may be "rejected or simply not understood" if it conflicts with a reader's frame (168). Hypothetically, I would apply this notion to formal as well as situational frames.
3. Cf., for example, Kenneth Burke, "Lexicon Rhetoricae," in *Counter-Statement*; Keith Fort, "Form, Authority, and the Critical Essay"; Richard Ohmann, "Freshman Composition and Administered Thought" (*English in America*, chap. 6); Coe, "An Apology for Form."

   It is important to emphasize that, for the classical rhetoricians, this department included critical judgment—selection among the invented materials—as well as organization. This, therefore, is the department most directly associated with logic and dialectic. It is also worth noting that there is some significant theory about basic patterns of development, founded largely on the insights of I. A. Richards and Burke. See Frank D'Angelo, *A Conceptual Theory of Rhetoric*, for example; see also Coe, *Form and Substance* (202–5, 278–80). But there is not at present adequate empirical evidence for deciding whether or not these basic patterns are commonly used to structure paragraphs or other short passages.

   De Beaugrande's discussion of text types and their role in reading comprehension is also relevant (chapter 7).

What we may loosely call "story grammars"—meaning not only the "grammars" devised for analyzing narratives (e.g., Rumelhart, Mandler and Johnson, Stein and Glenn) but also comparable "grammars" for other modes—chunk and label parts of the text, but they don't describe structure within small named parts. Most such "grammars" have this drawback.

4. See appendix B. Cf. Sandra Stotsky's criticism of Markels' "excessive reliance on bridging assumptions (words inferred by the reader) and transformational analyses" ("Review" 490) See also Alton Becker ("A Tagmemic Approach to Paragraph Analysis") and W. Ross Winterowd, *The Contemporary Writer* (113–15). It is worth noting, parenthetically, that there is a problem with Witte's term, "topical depth"—which is used to describe just those passages that composition teachers have traditionally described as lacking adequate development or "depth."

5. This quality allows natural language to "draw practically innumerable meanings from the finite set of lexical entities codified by the dictionary." Thus, says Ricoeur, natural language achieves "economy at the level of code" at the cost of "contextual dependence at the level of the message" (101). On one level, Ricoeur is here repeating de Saussure's assertion, "The value of . . . any term is . . . determined by its environment. . . . [I]t is quite clear that initially the concept is nothing, that is only a value determined by its relations with other similar values, and that without them the signification would not exist. . . . Proof of this is that the value of a term may be modified . . . solely because a neighboring term has been modified" (116–18). On another level, Ricoeur's point is that meaning is created by *words in communicative context*, which is one definition of discourse. Cf. Richards' attack on the "Proper Meaning Superstition" (8–12).

6. Rodgers usefully reminds us "that the paragraph (from Greek *para*, 'beside,' + *graphos*, 'mark') began as a punctuation device, a symbol placed in the margin to indicate a noteworthy break in the flow of discourse; only later did the word come to signify the stretch of language between breaks" ("A Discourse-Centered Rhetoric" 4). Indeed, as Edwin Herbert Lewis pointed out nearly a century ago, "The paragraph is the oldest mark of punctuation in Greek manuscripts. . . . It indicated that a sentence, or some longer division of the text, was *ended* in the underscored line. The mark thus distinguished the close of one section rather than the beginning of another" (9; emphasis added). Paragraphing in this sense literally defines (Latin: *de-* + *finire*), marks the end of some functionally or conceptually unified set of sentences. Or to shift the emphasis somewhat, paragraphing marks *boundaries*, not beginnings *or* endings as such. And only because, like other punc-

tuation marks, it signals boundaries does paragraphing come to define what lies within.

Rodgers' distinction between paragraph indents and what they signal is paralleled by Lackstrom, Selinker, and Trimble's distinction between conceptual and physical paragraphs, which is pedagogically clear and useful despite problematic tautologies implicit in their definitions.

7. For a particularly female version of Richards' metaphor, cf. Gertrude Stein's comparison of the writing process with forming a child in the womb during pregnancy (for a full quotation, see Coe, *Form and Substance* 32). Ann Berthoff adds, "'Womb' is superior to 'can' because it is a *dialectical* container" (personal communication, 1986). That is, womb and baby interact: though in one sense we may say the womb forms the baby, it is also responsive, also adapts to the becoming baby.

Half a century later, these metaphors have a significant added connotation, for we are very aware that plants grow in ecosystems, that wombs are affected by mothers' environments (often polluted and/or stressed). Richards' and Stein's organic metaphors become ecosystemic—and ecosystemic metaphors are useful because they shift our attention and emphasis from texts to the relationships between texts and contexts. Cf. Coe, "Eco-Logic" and "Closed System Composition," Matalene (789–91), and Cooper; cf. also Harris.

8. See Burke, "What Are the Signs of What? (A Theory of Entitlement)" and "Terministic Screens" in *Language as Symbolic Action*. I suggest *terministic motives* (rather than "screens") both to parallel *formal motives* and to avoid the passive process connoted by "screens."

9. Cf. Besner, Coe ("An Apology for Form"). Without necessarily endorsing his entire analysis, we can use James Berlin's distinction between expressionist and New Rhetorical process approaches ("Contemporary Composition") to inform the preceding analysis. For some previous work on the process relation between form and substance, see Coe, "Closed System Composition" and "Rhetoric 2001"; D'Angelo, *A Conceptual Theory of Rhetoric*; Keith Fort, "Form, Authority, and the Critical Essay"; Richard Ohmann, "Writing, Out in the World," in his *English in America*.

10. "A Generative Rhetoric of the Sentence" (157). It is also worth noting that levels of generality are "stepped," not continuous; that is why Christensen compares them with layers. It is levels of generality that should be referred to as a "ladder" (not the abstract-concrete continuum, which is, theoretically, continuous).

11. Significantly, computer music programs may be better adapted than mathematical programs for representing and analyzing the discourse matrix. This is because the analysis involves looking for analogous patterns in contexts where absolute values differ. For discussion of the

underlying conceptual distinction, analog/digital, see Bateson (364–78), Watzlawick, Beavin, and Jackson (60–67, 99–107), and Wilden (chap. 7).

12. For the initial definition and discussion of T-units, including the rationale for preferring T-units to sentences as a unit of analysis, see Hunt. A T-unit (or terminable unit) is a string of words that *could* be punctuated as a sentence. Thus except in the case of compound sentences, which contain two or more completely stated propositions and hence could be punctuated as two or more sentences, a T-unit is ordinarily the same as a sentence. Psycholinguistically, there is a sense in which an English T-unit usually is taken as a single statement to be transferred from short-term to long-term memory. (This hypothesis seems not to work in Chinese, however—which indicates the general danger of generalizing about writing from research done entirely on English composition.)

13. The précis is an interesting pedagogy. On one level, its prevalence may be explained by the need of the British Empire for middle-level administrators who could summarize their subordinates' reports accurately before passing them up the bureaucratic hierarchy. On another level, writing précis taught students to distinguish statements according to level of generality and to perceive the same sorts of cognitive structures identified by the discourse matrix. This is also, incidentally, a significant example of the relationship between a rhetorical form (the précis), a rhetorical process, and a cognitive process. A rhetorical form is, in a crucial sense, a synchronic embodiment (a memory, if you will) of the rhetorical and cognitive processes that produced it. The teaching of this rhetorical form, moreover, was a means of developing the cognitive ability. Cf. "The Rise of English" in Terry Eagleton's *Literary Theory* for a discussion of the social function of English studies as a discipline in English universities.

14. In "The Grammar of Coherence," W. Ross Winterowd asserts that

> there are seven relationships that prevail among T-units and, I would argue, in any stretch of discourse that is perceived as coherent. I have called these relationships (1) coordinate, (2) observative, (3) causative, (4) conclusive, (5) alternative, (6) inclusive, and (7) sequential. These relationships can be either *expressed* or *implied*. They are expressed in a variety of ways: through coordinating conjunctions, transitional adverbs, and a variety of other moveable modifiers. Just how they are implied remains a mystery. (228–29)

In matrix terms, causativity and inclusivity are varieties of subordination. Coordination, obversativity, alternativity, and sequence are varieties of coordination because they are all relationships among statements on the same level of generality. Depending upon whether it is deductive or inductive, conclusivity may constitute either subordination or superordination.

It is possible to make other divisions. Robert Bander, for example, argues that there are at least nine types of transitions: explanation, emphasis, qualification, illustration, comparison, contrast, concession, consequence, and summation (19–24). Any such theory which defines the relationships between conjunctive textual signals and semantic "movements of mind" suggests possible pedagogical responses to complaints such as Ann Berthoff's that the way "transition words" are commonly taught encourages "papers full of roadsigns pointing in the wrong direction—*however*, when there is no *however* relationship; *on the other hand*, introducing a faulty parallel; redundancy (the uninstructed writer's only means of emphasis); end linkages—which I call Nixonian Syntactic Ligature—with the beginning of each sentence picking up the exact wording of the end of the preceding sentence" ("Is Teaching Still Possible?" 746).

15. Ambiguities such as the two just discussed lead me to ask whether Christensen was entirely right in his implicit assertion that relationships among levels of generality are always the same as patterns of modification, and in particular whether the modifier is always more specific than what it modifies. If not, "level of generality" may not be quite the right title for the salient feature Christensen identified; in that case, Nold and Davis' explicit assertion that subordination, coordination, and superordination can be identified with particular "rhetorical operations" would also need to be revised. As already noted, Nold and Davis presume that propositions which define, exemplify, qualify, or give reasons are always more specific than (i.e., subordinate to) the statements they thus modify; that statements which restate, contradict, conjoin, or contrast are always at the same level of generality (i.e., coordinate); and that statements which generalize, draw inductive conclusions, or initiate a new subtopic are always at a higher level of generality (i.e., superordinate). Although these assumptions are close to some essential insight, they may constitute an overgeneralization. The relationship between cohesion cues (in the case being analyzed above, the shift from semicolons to a period and a new sentence) and the semantic structure of the text itself also needs further study. These ambiguities do not call Christensen's whole thesis about patterns of modification into question, but they do indicate places where it may need to be refined.

16. The students doing such exercises collect a sample of good examples (usually ten) of the type of writing they wish to learn. Using a combination of intuitive and explicit matrix analysis, as well as a variety of other

queries, they discover for themselves which discourse patterns predominate and hypothesize rhetorical purposes that explain the predominance. Not only does this empirical experience help them learn the particular type of writing (and learn it much better than if the instructor explained it to them), but it also teaches them how to teach themselves other types of writing in the future. (Coe "A Heuristic"; cf. Brosnahan et al.)

17. Two analyses of variance (ANOVA) were performed on the coded results, the first using total scores, the second using scores for each criterion. The significance level was set at $p = 0.05$. Three comparisons were done: traditional instruction group vs. matrix instruction group; matrix lecturer group vs. neutral instructor subgroup; traditional lecturer group vs. neutral instructor subgroup. On the first ANOVA (for total score), the groups were not significantly different before instruction with $p = 0.200$, $p = 0.238$ and $p = 0.107$ on the three comparisons. The matrix instruction group improved their total scores from a mean of 2.09 (standard deviation, 1.0874) to a mean of 3.1366 (standard deviation, 1.2948). The traditional instruction group improved their total scores from a mean of 1.6811 (standard deviation, 1.0682) to a mean of 2.0817 (standard deviation, 1.534). The probability of this occurring through a random sampling error was zero. The insignificance of the contrasts with the subgroups supervised by the neutral instructor was indicated by probabilities of $p = 0.464$ and $p = 0.624$ respectively.

On posttest contrasts, the mean scores of the matrix instruction group were higher than those of the traditional instruction group on each criterion (criterion 1: mean 0.7475 vs. 0.5849; criterion 2: mean 0.4220 vs. 0.1207; criterion 3: mean 0.8872 vs. 0.8213; criterion 3: mean 0.8872 vs. 0.8213; criterion 4: mean 0.7426 vs. 0.1530; criterion 5: mean 0.6072 vs. 3255). The data were significant on idea strings ($p = 0.001$), on only coordination and subordination within idea strings ($p = 0.001$), and on appropriate closings ($p = 0.003$). (See Fahey "Discourse Matrix Analysis.")

18. Cf. Reid. Kaplan's thesis, as he admits, is more suggestive than definitive: it does describe the problem, but suggests only directions and tentative solutions. Kaplan also, unfortunately, chose to frame his discussion with a set of questionable quotations from the Sapir-Whorf tradition; fortunately, however, his thesis does not actually depend on the Sapir-Whorf hypothesis.

19. A T-unit, by definition, contains one main proposition (i.e., the proposition represented by the main clause); but it may also contain subordinate clauses, hence secondary propositions (normally on a lower level of generality). Ordinarily, in matrix analysis, the T-unit is classified according to the level of generality of its main clause, thus avoiding exces-

sive complexity. In principle, however, the clause has the tightest boundaries for isolating propositions. Given the differing natures of Chinese and English syntax, Chen argues that the clause provides a more appropriate basis of comparison. (Cf. Lu Shu-xiang's discussion of the appropriateness of using clauses as analytical units in Chinese linguistics.)

Chen defined a clause as a grammatical unit containing all the components of a complete logical proposition: in semantics, an understood topic slot plus a comment slot; in syntax, a subject (possibly elliptical) slot plus the obligatory finite predicate slot, as well as any optional phrasal modifiers. Units containing all these elements and beginning with a relative pronoun, however, were defined as clauses only when appositive. And infinitivals, which linguists sometimes interpret as clauses with omitted subjects, Chen defined as phrases.

20. The effects of language and political stance on the sample editorials were analyzed by two-way multivariate analyses. Forty newspaper editorials were divided into four cells (Chinese-communist, Chinese-capitalist, English-communist, English-capitalist) and analyzed statistically at 0.05 level of significance. Two-way multivariate analysis of the ratio of number of node strings to number of clauses, the only macrolevel variable homogeneous across all four cells, revealed that language was a significant influence ($F=6.976$, $p = 0.012$) while political stance was not.

At the microlevel, political stance was found to have a significant effect on the number of subtopics per node string ($F = 6.870$, $p = 0.013$), clauses per node string ($F = 5.260$, $p = 0.028$), and levels of generality per idea string ($F = 5.944$, $p = 0.020$). Language had a significant effect on the average number of clauses per idea string ($F = 22.135$). But there was no significant interaction between language and political stance on any of the four variables.

Chinese editorials had more coordinate structures (indicated by length of node string) and more elaborating details (indicated by the number of clauses per idea string). Communist editorials in either language had a greater range of development (indicated by number of subtopics per node string), but capitalist newspapers had more elaborating details (indicated by the number of clauses per node string) and also a greater depth of development (indicated by the number of levels of generality per idea string).

21. In fact, the matrix diagram's most significant drawback involves people who feel secure with words but insecure with diagrams. Fortunately, relatively few composition students have this learning disability and insecurity; unfortunately, many English teachers do. (And teachers, unlike students, usually have the power to refuse to learn something they

find difficult.) Despite the matrix's demonstrated effectiveness in that context, one technical institute removed from its curriculum a unit based on the matrix—because it was not immediately comprehensible to the instructors (who, in fairness, have such a heavy work load—presently about 250 writing students each per semester—that they cannot entirely be blamed for wanting to stick with the familiar).

22. See *The Christensen Rhetoric Program* (lesson 1). It is interesting to juxtapose Christensen's notion (which I have dubbed "generative form") with Paulo Freire's notion of "generative themes." For a discussion and case study of Freire's concept as applied to teaching postsecondary composition students, see Fiore and Elsasser (both works listed). Cf. also Shor.

23. Shaughnessy's major example (250–56), based on a list from Richard Wright's *Black Boy*, works quite well, as does the exercise in Coe, *Form and Substance* (96–98). Cf. also Shor (chap. 5).

24. Cf. Kenneth Burke's assertion that "purely formal patterns can readily awaken an attitude of collaborative expectancy in us. For instance, imagine a passage built about a set of oppositions. . . . Once you grasp the trend of the form, it invites participation regardless of the subject matter. . . . Thus you are drawn to the form, not in your capacity as a partisan, but because of some 'universal' appeal in it" (*Rhetoric* 58; cf. Coe, "An Apology for Form").

25. Cf. Langer, *Philosophy in a New Key*, esp. chapters 4–5. I presume Langer chooses her term to emphasize the sense in which generalization is a type of abstracting—for her, one of two basic types.

26. In *The Philosophy of Rhetoric*, Richards writes,

> A sensation would be something that was just *so*, on its own, a datum; as such we have none. Instead we have perceptions, responses whose character comes to them from the past as well as the present occasion. A perception is never just of an *it*; perception takes whatever it perceives as a thing of a certain sort. . . . [W]e *begin* with the general abstract anything, split it as the world makes us, into sorts and then arrive at concrete particulars. . . . This bit of paper here now in my hand is a concrete particular to us so far as we think of it as paperish . . . ; it is the more concrete as we take it as more sorts, and the more specific as the sorts are narrower and more exclusive. (30–31)

As the Latin etymology suggests, there is a conceptual distinction between calling something a *datum* (i.e., a given) and calling it a *fact* (i.e., made, synthesized by an agent). Cf. Berthoff, ed., *Reclaiming the Imagination* (part 1); Lindemann, *A Rhetoric for Writing Teachers* (60–67); Coe, *Form and Substance* (204–27). To keep the two types of abstraction distinct in our minds, we might well remember Cole-

ridge's distinction between Primary Imagination (the basis of preconscious perception) and secondary imagination (the basis of conscious
interpretation)

27. Vygotsky's term is "scientific concept"; in the context of this discussion,
it is essentially equivalent to abstraction, not generalization (though it
involves both). Vygotsky's point has everything to do with why naming
matters (cf. Burke, "What Are the Signs of What?" in *Language*).
Vygotsky's distinction between pseudoconcepts and scientific concepts
allows us, moreover, to distinguish between the ability to attach an abstract label appropriately to an event and the ability to use an abstract
concept to gain insight into that event. Thus when an impressed jour-
nalist writes of a Filipino peasant's ability to say that his financial difficulties are a result of U.S. imperialism, we know that the peasant has
attached that abstract term to his concrete situation in a way which is
semantically correct and that he has made a connection between global
and local events. But we cannot yet be sure that he is using an abstract
understanding of imperialism to achieve a fuller or better understanding of his situation; he may just be using abstract language to label what
he already believed before he met the abstract term. Cf. Coe, "Chinese
Speak and Doublespeak" (6–7), and Stotsky's distinction, based in
Vygotsky, between "*how* words are used to create meaning in connected discourse" and *what* words are used ("Lexical Cohesion" 445).

28. See Witte, "Topical Structure & Revision" and "Topical Structure &
Writing Quality"; Faigley and Witte, "Analyzing Revision."

29. Personal communication, 1974. I use the term *formal dash* to distinguish a dash used for summation (usually after an introductory series)
from dashes used for emphasis, to enclose parenthetical elements, or to
indicate abrupt breaks in dialogue.

GLOSSARY

Abstraction: This term is used in at least four ways relevant to composition: (1) as a synonym for generalization; (2) to emphasize the sense in which all human perception and interpretation is an abstraction from reality (cf. Richards); (3) to discuss the ability to use abstract concepts to further interpretation (cf. Vygotsky); and (4) as a stylistic value (the antithesis of concrete), denoting words and phrases that do not evoke sensory images in readers' minds. This last use, most common in textbooks, refers to the abstract-concrete continuum, usually discussed as a simple dichotomy between abstract and concrete terms.

Ambiguity: That quality which allows more than one valid interpretation of a text or other communication (cf. Empson).

Conceptual paragraph: A vaguely defined term used to distinguish the cohesion cue of paragraph indentation (the "physical paragraph") from the semantic or functional denoted unit by paragraphing (cf. Lackstrom, Selinker, and Trimble).

Coordination: If a statement is on the same level of generality as the preceding statement—related to it by such rhetorical operations as contrasting, contradicting, conjoining, or repeating—we call it coordinate with that preceding statement. When diagrammed, it is to the right of and on the same level as the preceding statement.

Discourse: As Winograd points out, the term *discourse* has been used in linguistics alone to discuss some fifty phenomena. Widdowson stipulates this definition: "a use of sentences to perform acts of communication which cohere into larger communicative units, ultimately establishing a kind of rhetorical pattern which characterizes the piece of language as a whole as a kind of communication" (98). The term seems to have three important connotations: (1) it refers to language in communicative context; (2) ultimately, at least, it concerns whole communications; (3) although in certain odd cases a single sentence may constitute a whole discourse, the term normally refers to larger units of language (in Shaughnessy's phrase, "beyond the sentence"). Operationally, a particular discourse is defined by characteristic rhetorical patterns; functionally, it penetrates broader contexts, for which it has implications and in terms of which it must be explained (cf. Foucault, esp. 50–56). Though the emphasis here is on discourse as defined by characteristic patterns "beyond the sentence," the other connotations are pertinent to the processes of describing and explaining those patterns and their implications.

Discourse matrix: A technique for analyzing and diagramming the patterns of modification (among levels of generality) that constitute a key characteristic of the semantic structure of discursive discourse. Such a drawing is constructed by numbering each T-unit (or sentence or clause) and representing it by a circle. Level of generality is indicated on the drawing by the relative positions of the circles. (Cf. Nold and Davis.)

Idea string: A series of statements that represent the simple lineal development of a single "point," which is often found at the beginning of the string. Logically, an idea string is defined by the generalization that encompasses all the statements in the string. Operationally, one starts with a specific and traces back to the generalization; by definition, an intervening superordination breaks the string.

Level of generality: This term refers to the distinction treated in most textbooks as a simple dichotomy between general and specific (or particular). It is a characteristic of propositions or statements within a discourse, not a stylistic quality of language (insofar as ideas and words are separable). The level of generality of a particular concept or statement can be identified only relative to other ideas in the discourse. A more general idea logically encompasses a less general idea.

Node string: Two or more nonconsecutive units above the lowest level of generality related to each other by any type of coordination except restatement. Noting the number of nodes on a string is useful because it ordinarily indicates the number of subtopics mentioned in a passage (which is why restatements are excluded).

Stadium (pl. *stadia*): According to Rodgers, a series of sentences "containing a single topic, together with any accrete extensions or adjunctive support." Thus a stadium is a subordinate pattern within a discourse sequence that *could* be bounded by paragraph indents. How stadia correlate with paragraphs, superordinations, and idea strings remains to be discovered empirically.

Statement: A proposition understood by readers to be asserted by a text (written or oral). As an operational hypothesis, for ordinary purposes of discourse matrix analysis, presume one statement per T-unit.

Subordination: If a statement is less general than the preceding statement—related to it by such rhetorical operations as defining, exemplifying, giving a reason, deducing, qualifying, or explaining (i.e., making plain by restating more specifically)—we call it subordinate to that preceding statement. Conceptually, it is encompassed by the preceding statement. When diagrammed, it is to the right of and lower than the preceding statement.

Superordination; If a statement is more general than the preceding statement—related to it by such rhetorical operations as generalizing, commenting, or inferring a conclusion—we call it superordinate to that preceding statement. When diagrammed, it is to the right of and higher than the preceding statement.

T-unit: Terminable unit—an independent clause plus all sentence elements subordinated to it. Except in the case of compound sentences, which contain more than one independent clause (hence more than one T-unit), a T-unit is equivalent to a sentence, representing one main proposition. (Cf. Hunt.)

Works Cited

Starred items (*) constitute what has been dubbed above the "Christensen tradition" on *dispositio*. For a review of this literature, see pages 12–18 in chapter 2. The central early work in this tradition was reprinted in *The Sentence and the Paragraph*. Much of it has also been reprinted in such anthologies as Graves, *Rhetoric and Composition* (lst ed.); Tate and Corbett, *The Writing Teacher's Sourcebook*; and Winterowd, *Contemporary Rhetoric*.

Aristotle. *The Rhetoric*. Trans. Lane Cooper. Englewood Cliffs: Prentice-Hall, 1932.

Baker, Sheridan. *The Complete Stylist and Handbook*. New York: Crowell, 1976.

Bamberg, Betty. "What Makes a Text Coherent?" *College Composition and Communication* 34 (1983): 417–29.

Bander, Robert. *American English Rhetoric*. 2nd ed. New York: Holt, 1978.

Bateson, Gregory. *Steps to an Ecology of Mind*. New York: Ballantine, 1972.

Becker, Alton. "A Tagmemic Approach to Paragraph Analysis." *College Composition and Communication* 16 (1965): 237–42.

Bennett, James R., et al. "The Paragraph: An Annotated Bibliography." *Style* 9 (1977): 107–18.

Bereiter, Carl, and Marlene Scardamalia. "Written Composition." *Research on Writing*. 3rd ed. Ed. Peter Mosenthal, Lynne Tamor, and Sean A. Walmsley. London: Longman, 1984. 3–25.

Berlin, James. "Contemporary Composition: The Major Pedagogical Theories." *College English* 44 (1982): 765–77.

———. "Rhetoric and Literacy in American Colleges." *Oldspeak/ Newspeak Rhetorical Transformations.* Ed. Charles W. Kneupper. Arlington: Texas Rhetoric Society of America, 1985. 257–66.

Bernstein, Basel. *Class, Code, and Control.* London: Routledge and Kegan Paul, 1977.

Berthoff, Ann E. *Forming/Thinking/Writing: The Composing Imagination.* Upper Montclair: Boynton/Cook, 1982.

———. "The Intelligent Eye and the Thinking Hand." *The Writer's Mind: Writing as a Mode of Thinking.* Ed. Janice N. Hays, Phyllis A. Roth, Jon R. Ramsey, and Robert D. Foulke. Urbana: NCTE, 1983. 191–96.

———. "Is Teaching Still Possible? Writing, Meaning, and Higher Order Reasoning." *College English* 46 (1984): 743–55.

———, ed. *Reclaiming the Imagination: Philosophical Perspectives for Writers and Teachers of Writing.* Upper Montclair: Boynton/Cook, 1984.

Besner, Neil. "Process against Product: A Real Opposition?" *English Quarterly* 18 (1985): 9–16.

Bizzell, Patricia. "What Happens When Basic Writers Come to College?" *College Composition and Communication* 37 (1986): 294–301.

Blair, Hugh. *Lectures on Rhetoric and Belles Lettres.* Ed. Harold F. Harding. Carbondale: Southern Illinois UP, 1965.

Braddock, Richard. "The Frequency and Placement of Topic Sentences in Expository Prose." *Research in the Teaching of English* 8 (1974): 287–302.

Britton, James, et al. *The Development of Writing Abilities (11–18).* London: Macmillan Education, 1975.

Brosnahan, Irene. "Chinese Assumptions about the Reading Process: Implications for Teaching." Conference on College Composition and Communication. Detroit, March 1983.

Brosnahan, Irene, Richard Coe, and Ann Johns. "Discourse Analysis of Written Texts in an Overseas Teacher Training Program." *English Quarterly* 20 (1987): 16–25.

*Brostoff, Anita. "Coherence: 'Next to' Is Not 'Connected To.'" *College Composition and Communication* 32 (1981): 278–94.

Bruffee, Kenneth A. "Writing and Reading as Collaborative Social Acts." *The Writer's Mind: Writing as a Mode of Thinking.* Ed. Janice N. Hays, Phyllis A. Roth, Jon R. Ramsey, and Robert D. Foulke. Urbana: NCTE, 1983. 159–70.

Burke, Kenneth. *Counter-Statement*. 1931. Berkeley: U of California P, 1968.

———. *A Grammar of Motives*. 1945. Berkeley: U of California P, 1969.

———. *Language as Symbolic Action: Essays on Life, Literature, and Method*. Berkeley: U of California P, 1966.

———. *The Philosophy of Literary Form*. Rev. ed. New York: Vintage, 1957.

———. *A Rhetoric of Motives*. 1950. Berkeley: U of California P, 1969.

*Caplan, Rebekah, and Catharine Keech. *Showing-Writing: A Training Program to Help Students Be Specific*. Berkeley: Bay Area Writing Project Collaborative Research Study No. 2, 1980.

Chafe, Wallace. "The Deployment of Consciousness in the Production of a Narrative." *The Pear Stories: Cognitive, Cultural, and Linguistic Aspects of Narrative Production*. Norwood: Ablex, 1981. 9–50.

Chen, Sun-I. "Argumentative Discourse Structure in Chinese and English Writing: A Comparative Analysis." M.A. thesis: Simon Fraser U, 1986.

———. "A Comparative Analysis of Paragraph Structures in Chinese and English." Unpublished paper. Simon Fraser U, 1983.

*Christensen, Francis. "A Generative Rhetoric of the Paragraph." *College Composition and Communication* 16 (1965): 144–56.

*———. "A Generative Rhetoric of the Sentence." *College Composition and Communication* 14 (1963): 155–61.

*Christensen, Francis, and Bonnijean Christensen. *Notes toward a New Rhetoric: Nine Essays for Teachers*. New York: Harper, 1978.

*———. *A New Rhetoric*. New York: Harper, 1976.

**The Christensen Rhetoric Program*. New York: Harper, 1968.

Christie, Frances. "Language and Schooling." *Language, Schooling and Society*. Ed. Stephen Tchudi. Upper Montclair: Boynton, 1985. 21–40.

Cicero. *De Inventione*. Trans. G. L. Hendrickson. Cambridge: Harvard UP, 1939.

Coe, Richard M. "An Apology for Form; or, Who Took the Form Out of the Process?" *College English* 49 (1987): 13–28.

———. "Chinese Speak and Doublespeak." *Quarterly Review of Doublespeak* 12.2–3 (1986): 6–7, 10–11.

———. "Closed System Composition." *ETC., A Review of General Semantics* 32 (1975): 403–12.

———. "Eco-Logic for the Composition Classroom." *College Composition and Communication* 16 (1975): 232–37.

———. *Form and Substance: An Advanced Rhetoric.* New York: Wiley; Scott, 1981.

———. "A Heuristic for Analyzing a Particular Type of Writing Prior to Learning How to Produce It." ERIC 1984. ED 257 105.

———. "Rhetoric 2001." *Freshman English News* 3.1 (Spring 1974): 1–13.

Cooper, Marilyn. "The Ecology of Writing." *College English* 48 (1986): 364–75.

Corbett, Edward P. J. *Classical Rhetoric for the Modern Student.* 2nd ed. New York: Oxford UP, 1971.

———. *The Little English Handbook: Choices and Conventions.* 4th ed. Glenview: Scott, 1984.

*D'Angelo, Frank. *A Conceptual Theory of Rhetoric.* Cambridge: Winthrop, 1975.

*———. "A Generative Rhetoric of the Essay." *College Composition and Communication* 25 (1974): 388–96.

———. "Modes of Discourse." *Teaching Composition: Ten Bibliographic Essays.* Ed. Gary Tate. Forth Worth: Texas Christian UP, 1976. 111–35.

———. "The Topic Sentence Revisited." *College Composition and Communication* 27 (1986): 431–41.

de Beaugrande, Robert. *Text, Discourse, and Process: Toward a Multidisciplinary Science of Texts.* Norwood: Ablex, 1980.

de Castell, Suzanne, Allan Luke, and Kieran Egan, eds,. *Literacy, Society, and Schooling: A Reader.* Cambridge: Cambridge UP, 1986.

de Saussure, Ferdinand. *Course in General Linguistics.* Ed. Charles Bally and Albert Sechehaye with Albert Riedlinger. Trans. Wade Baskin. New York: McGraw-Hill, 1966.

Eagleton, Terry. *Literary Theory: An Introduction.* Oxford: Blackwell, 1983.

Eden, Rick, and Ruth Mitchell. "Paragraphing for the Reader." *College Composition and Communication* 27 (1986): 416–30.

Empson, William. *Seven Types of Ambiguity.* 3rd ed. New York: New Directions, n.d.

Fahey, Susan. "An Analysis of Technical Writing Using the Nold and Davis Discourse Matrix." Unpublished paper. Simon Fraser U, 1982.

———. "Discourse Matrix Analysis: Empirical Evaluation of a Sample Pedagogy." M.A. thesis: Simon Fraser U, 1986.

Fahnestock, Jeanne. "Semantic and Lexical Coherence." *College Composition and Communication* 34 (1983): 400–416.

Faigley, Lester, and Stephen Witte. "Analyzing Revision." *College Composition and Communication* 32 (1981): 400–414.

Fillmore, Charles. "An Alternative to Checklist Theories of Meaning." *Proceedings of the First Annual Meeting of the Berkeley Linguistics Society.* Berkeley: Institute of Human Learning, 1975. 123–31.

Fiore, Kyle, and Nan Elsasser. "'Strangers No More': A Liberatory Literacy Curriculum." *College English* 44 (1982): 115–28.

———. "Through Writing We Transform Our World: Third World Women and Literacy." *Humanities in Society* 4 (1981): 395–418.

Flower, Linda, et al. "Detection, Diagnosis, and the Strategies of Revision." *College Composition and Communication* 37 (1986): 16–55.

Fort, Keith. "Form, Authority, and the Critical Essay." *College English* 33 (1971): 629–39.

Foucault, Michel. *The Archaeology of Knowledge and the Discourse on Language.* Trans. A. M. Sheridan Smith. New York: Pantheon, 1982.

Freedman, Sarah, and Ellen Nold. "The Ladder of Abstraction." Unpublished paper. Stanford U, 1976.

Freire, Paulo. *Education for Critical Consciousness.* 1973; New York: Continuum, 1986.

Goetz, Ernest T., and Bonnie B. Armbruster. "Psychological Correlates of Text Structure." *Theoretical Issues in Reading Comprehension.* Ed. Rand J. Spiro, Bertram C. Bruce, and William F. Brewer. Hillsdale: Erlbaum, 1980. 201–20.

Goffman, Erving. *Frame Analysis.* New York: Harper, 1974.

*Grady, Michael. "A Conceptual Rhetoric of the Composition." *College Composition and Communication* 22 (1971): 348–54.

*———. "On Teaching Christensen Rhetoric." *English Journal* 61 (1972): 859–73, 877.

Graves, Richard L., ed. *Rhetoric and Composition: A Sourcebook for Teachers.* New Rochelle: Hayden, 1976.

Gutwinski, Waldemar. *Cohesion in Literary Texts: A Study of Some Grammatical and Lexical Features of English Discourse.* The Hague: Mouton, 1976.

Halliday, M. A. K., and R. Hasan. *Cohesion in English.* London: Longman, 1976.

Harris, Wendell V. "Toward an Ecological Criticism: Contextual versus Unconditioned Literary Theory." *College English* 48 (1982): 116–31.

Haswell, Richard H. "The Organization of Impromptu Essays." *College Composition and Communication* 37 (1986): 402–15.

Hayakawa, S. I. *Language in Thought and Action.* 3rd ed. 1939; New York: Harcourt, 1972.

Hessami, Irene. "Comparative Analysis of Persian and English Discourse." Unpublished paper. Simon Fraser U, 1983.

Hunt, Kellogg W. "A Synopsis of Clause-to-Sentence Length Factors." *English Journal* 54 (1965): 300, 305–9.

Jia Shan. "Contrastive Discourse Structure in English and Chinese." Unpublished paper. Shanghai Foreign Language Institute, 1982.

Kaplan, Robert. "Cultural Thought Patterns in Inter-Cultural Education." *Language Learning* 16 (1966): 1–20.

* Karrfalt, David H. "Generation of Paragraphs and Larger Units." *College Composition and Communication* 17 (1966): 82–87.

* Keech, Catharine. "Apparent Regression in Student Writing Performance as a Function of Unrecognized Changes in Task Complexity." Diss. U of California, Berkeley, 1984.

Kinneavy, James L. *A Theory of Discourse.* Englewood Cliffs: Prentice, 1971.

Kintsch, Walter. "On Modeling Comprehension." *Literacy, Society, and Schooling: A Reader.* Ed. Suzanne de Castell, Allan Luke, and Kieran Egan. Cambridge: Cambridge UP, 1986. 175–95.

Kintsch, Walter, and T[eun] A. van Dijk. "Towards a Model of Text Comprehension and Production." *Psychological Review* 85 (1978): 363–94.

Kintsch, Walter, and Douglas Vipond. "Reading Comprehension and Readability in Educational Practice and Psychological Theory." *Perspectives on Memory Research.* Ed. Lars-Goran Nilsson. Hillsdale: Erlbaum, 1979. 329–65.

Kuhn, Thomas S. *The Structure of Scientific Revolutions.* 2nd ed. Chicago: U of Chicago P, 1970.

Lackstrom, John E., Larry Selinker, and Louis P. Trimble. "Technical Rhetorical Principles and Grammatical Choice." *A TEFL Anthology: Selected Articles from the English Teaching Forum, 1973–78.* Washington: International Communications Agency [USIA], 1980. 258–63.

Langer, Susanne K. *Mind: An Essay on Human Feeling.* Baltimore: Johns Hopkins UP, 1967.

———. *Philosophy in a New Key.* 1942. New York: Pelican, 1948.

Larson, Richard L. "Structure and Form in Non-Fiction Prose." *Teaching Composition: Ten Bibliographic Essays.* Ed. Gary Tate. Forth Worth: Texas Christian UP, 1976. 45–71.

———. "Toward a Linear Rhetoric of the Essay." *College Composition and Communication* 22 (1971): 140–46.

LeFevre, Karen Burke. *Invention as a Social Act.* Carbondale: Southern Illinois UP, 1986.

Lewis, Edwin Herbert. *The History of the English Paragraph.* Chicago: U of Chicago P, 1894.

Lindemann, Erika. *A Rhetoric for Writing Teachers.* New York: Oxford, 1982.

Long Won-guang, "On the Semantic Structure of Expository Discourse." Unpublished paper. Shanghai Foreign Language Institute, 1982.

Lu, Min-zhao. "From Silence to Words: Writing as Struggle." *College English* 49 (1987): 437–48.

Lu Shu-xiang. *Chung-Kuo Wen-Fa Yiao-Lueh* [Chinese Grammar]. Shanghai: Shang-Wu, 1954.

Lu Zheng-wei. "The Conceptual Paragraph, Physical Paragraph, Stadium and Their Relationship." Unpublished paper. Shanghai Foreign Language Institute, 1982.

Mandler, J. M., and N. S. Johnson. "Remembrance of Things Parsed: Story Structure and Recall." *Cognitive Psychology* 9 (1977): 111–51.

Markels, Robin Bell. "Cohesion Paradigms in Paragraphs." *College English* 45 (1983): 450–64.

———. *A New Perspective on Cohesion in Expository Paragraphs.* Carbondale: Southern Illinois UP, 1984.

Matalene, Carolyn. "Contrastive Rhetoric: An American Writing Teacher in China." *College English* 47 (1985): 789–808.

Meade, Richard A., and W. Geiger Ellis. "Paragraph Development in the Modern Age of Rhetoric." *English Journal* 59 (1970): 219–26.

Needham, Joseph. *Science and Civilization in China.* Vol. 2. 1956; Cambridge: Cambridge UP, 1962.

Ning Yi-zhong. "A Preliminary Study of the Internal Structure of English Magazine Journalism." Unpublished paper. Shanghai Foreign Language Institute, 1982.

*Nold, Ellen W., and Brent E. Davis. "The Discourse Matrix." *College Composition and Communication* 31 (1980): 141–52.

Ohmann, Richard. *English in America.* New York: Oxford, 1976.

———. "Use Definite, Specific, Concrete Language." *College English* 41 (1979): 390–97.

Perl, Sondra. "Understanding Composing." *College Composition and Communication* 31 (1980): 363–69.

Phelps, Louise Wetherbee. "Dialectics of Coherence: Toward an Integrative Theory." *College English* 47 (1985): 12–29.

*Pitkin, Willis. "Discourse Blocs." *College Composition and Communication* 20 (1969): 138–48.

Project Literacy Staff Development Manual. Huntington Beach: Huntington Beach School District, n.d.

Quintilian. *Institutio Oratoria.* Trans. H. E. Butler. London: Heineman, 1922.

Reid, Joy M. "English Composition: The Linear Product of American Thought." *College Composition and Communication* 35 (1984): 449–52.

Reither, James A. "Writing and Knowing: Toward Redefining the Writing Process." *College English* 47 (1985): 620–28.

Richards, I. A. *The Philosophy of Rhetoric.* London: Oxford, 1936.

Ricoeur, Paul. "Creativity in Language: Word, Polysemy, Metaphor." *Philosophy Today* 17 (1973): 97–111.

Rodgers, Paul. "Alexander Bain and the Rise of the Organic Paragraph." *Quarterly Journal of Speech* 58 (1965): 408–17.

*———. "A Discourse-Centered Rhetoric of the Paragraph." *College Composition and Communication* 17 (1966): 2–11.

*———. "The Stadium of Discourse." *College Composition and Communication* 18 (1967): 178–85.

Rumelhart, David E. "Understanding and Summarizing Brief Stories." *Basic Processes in Reading: Perception and Comprehension.* Ed. David Laberge and S. Jay Samuels. Hillsdale: Erlbaum, 1977. 265–303.

The Sentence and the Paragraph. Urbana: NCTE, 1966.

*Shaughnessy, Mina. *Errors and Expectations.* New York: Oxford, 1977.

Shor, Ira. *Critical Teaching and Everyday Life.* Boston: South End, 1980.

Sloan, Gary. "The Frequency of Transitional Markers in Discursive Prose." *College English* 46 (1984): 158–79.

———. "Transitions: Relationships among T-units." *College Composition and Communication* 34 (1983): 447–53.

Sommers, Nancy. "Revision Strategies of Student Writers and Experienced Adult Writers." *College Composition and Communication* 31 (1980): 378–88.

Stein, Nancy L., and Christine G. Glenn. "An Analysis of Story Comprehension in Elementary School Children." *New Directions in Dis-*

course Processing. Vol. 2. Ed. Roy O. Freedle. Norwood: Ablex, 1979.
53–120.

Stotsky, Sandra. Rev. of *A New Perspective on Cohesion in Expository Paragraphs* by Robin Bell Markels. *College Composition and Communication*
37 (1986): 489–90.

————. "Types of Lexical Cohesion in Expository Writing: Implications for
Developing the Vocabulary of Academic Discourse." *College Composition and Communication* 34 (1983): 430–46.

Strunk, William, Jr., and E. B. White. *The Elements of Style.* New York:
Macmillan, 1959.

Tannen, Deborah. "What's in a Frame? Surface Evidence for Underlying
Expectations." *New Directions in Discourse Processing.* Vol. 2. Ed. Roy
O. Freedle. Norwood: Ablex, 1979. 137–81.

Tate, Gary, ed. *Teaching Composition: Ten Bibliographical Essays.* Fort
Worth: Texas Christian UP, 1976.

Tate, Gary and Edward P. J. Corbett, eds. *The Writing Teacher's Sourcebook*
New York: Oxford, 1981.

van Dijk, Teun A., and Walter Kintsch. *Strategies of Discourse Comprehension.* New York: Academic, 1983.

Vygotsky, L. S. *Thought and Language.* Ed. and trans. E. Hartman and G.
Vakar. Cambridge: MIT, 1962

Watzlawick, Paul, Janet Beavin, and Don Jackson. *Pragmatics of Human
Communication.* New York: Norton, 1967.

Wayne, Don E. *Penshurst: The Semiotics of Place and the Poetics of History.* Madison: U of Wisconsin P, 1984.

Widdowson, H. G. *Explorations in Linguistics.* Oxford: Oxford UP, 1979.

Wilden, Anthony. *System and Structure.* London: Tavistock, 1972.

Winograd, T. "A Framework for Understanding Discourse." *Cognitive Processes in Communication.* Ed. P. Carpenter and M. Just. Hillsdale:
Erlbaum, 1977.

Winterowd, W. Ross. "Beyond Style." *Philosophy and Rhetoric* 5 (Spring
1972): 88–110. Rpt. *Contemporary Rhetoric.* Ed. Winterowd. 206–25.

————, ed. *Contemporary Rhetoric: A Conceptual Background with Readings.* New York: Harcourt, 1975.

————. *The Contemporary Writer.* New York: Harcourt, 1975.

————. "The Grammar of Coherence." *College English* 32 (1970): 828–35.
Rpt. *Contemporary Rhetoric.* Ed. Winterowd. 225–33.

Witte, Stephen. "Topical Structure and Revision: An Exploratory Study."
College Composition and Communication 34 (1983): 313–41.

————. "Topical Structure and Writing Quality: Some Possible Text-Based Explanations of Reader's Judgments of Student Writing." *Visible Language* 17 (1983): 177–205.

Wu Jing-rong, Ding Wan-da, and Qian Qing, eds. *Readings in Modern English Prose.* Beijing: Shang-wu, 1982.

Xu Yong-hui, "Unity of English Paragraphs and the Discourse Matrix." Unpublished paper. Shanghai Foreign Language Institute, 1982.

Zhu Wei-fang. "Discourse Analysis in Language Teaching." Unpublished paper. Beijing Foreign Language Institute, 1985.

————. "Using the Discourse Matrix to Analyze the Semantic Structure of Some Expository Prose." Unpublished paper. Shanghai Foreign Language Institute, 1982.

Author Index

Albee, Edward, xi
Aristotle, 19
Armbruster, Bonnie, 7, 8
Augustine, 60

Baker, Sheridan, 88
Bamberg, Betty, 8, 17
Bander, Robert, 53, 101n.14
Bateson, Gregory, 100n.11
Beavin, Janet, 100n.11
Becker, Alton, 9, 98n.4
Bereiter, Carl, 5
Berlin, James, 75, 99n.9
Berthoff, Ann, xiii, 7, 9, 41, 42,
    79–80, 81, 99n.7, 101n.14,
    104n.26
Besner, Neil, 99n.9
Bizzell, Patricia, 53
Braddock, Richard, 44, 56
Brosnahan, Irene, xiv, 68, 69–70,
    102n.16
Bruffee, Kenneth, 53
Burke, Kenneth, 5, 11, 15, 20, 21,
    23, 53, 73, 76, 97nn.2, 3, 99n.8,
    104n.24, 105n.27

Caplan, Rebekah, 15, 68
Chen, Sun-I, xiii, 54, 56–59,
    103n.19

Christensen, Francis, ix, 3, 12–18,
    20, 22, 24, 25, 26, 27, 28, 33, 34,
    35, 40, 46, 65, 66, 68, 69, 76, 93,
    95, 99n.10, 101n.15, 104n.22
Christie, Frances, 75
Cicero, 60
Coleridge, Samuel, 104n.26
Cooper, Marilyn, 99n.7
Corbett, Edward, xiv, 93, 111

D'Angelo, Frank, 5, 12, 19, 97n.3,
    99n.9
Davis, Brent, 3, 14, 15, 16, 33, 34,
    37, 39–40, 55, 56, 83–86, 91,
    94, 95, 101n.15, 108
de Beaugrand, Robert, 97nn.2, 3
de Saussure, Ferdinand, 98n.5

Eagleton, Terry, 100n.13
Eden, Rick, 15, 17, 49
Elsasser, Nan, 104n.22
Empson, William, 11, 107
Evans, Bergan, 35, 93

Fahey, Susan, xiii, 49–52, 67, 68
Faigley, Lester, 105n.28
Faulkner, William, 13–14
Fiore, Kyle, 104n.22

Flower, Linda, 5
Fort, Keith, 97n.3, 99n.9
Foucault, Michel, 10, 73, 74–75,
    82, 108
Freedman, Sarah, 15
Freire, Paulo, 104n.22

Glenn, Christine, 98n.3
Goetz, Ernest, 7, 8
Goffman, Ernest, 97n.2
Grady, Michael, 12
Graves, Richard, 111
Gutierrez, Kris, 66

Harris, Wendell, 99n.7
Hayakawa, S. I., 22
Hessami, Irene, 54, 60–61
Hunt, Kellogg, 109

Isocrates, 53

Jackson, Don, 100n.11
Jia Shan, xiii, 54–55, 59, 67
Johnson, N. S., 98n.3
Johnson, Samuel, 20

Kaplan, Robert, 54, 102n.18
Karrfalt, David, 14, 33, 39, 40
Keech, Catharine, 15, 68
Kintsch, Walter, 6, 16, 18, 34, 97n.2
Kipling, Rudyard, 28
Kuhn, Thomas, 76

Lackstrom, John, 99n.6, 107
Langer, Susanne, 79, 104n.25
Larson, Richard, xiv, 6–7
LeFevre, Karen Burke, xii, xiii, 75

Lewis, Edwin Herbert, 98n.6
Lindemann, Erika, xiv, 104n.26
Long Won-guang, 45, 47
Lu, Min-zhao, 44
Lu Shu-xiang, 103n.19
Lu Zheng-wei, 45, 47

Mandler, J. M., 98n.3
Mao Ze-dung, 54, 55
Markels, Robin Bell, 8, 9, 10, 36,
    97n.2, 98n.4
Matalene, Carolyn, 44, 99n.7
Memering, Dean, xiv, 68, 69,
    91–92
Michell, Ruth, 15, 17, 49
Michener, James, xii

Needham, Joseph, 47, 60
Ning Yi-zhong, xiii, 48–49
Nold, Ellen, xi, 3, 14, 15, 16, 33,
    34, 37, 39–40, 55, 56, 83–86,
    91, 94, 95, 101n.15, 108

Ohmann, Richard, 76, 82, 97n.3,
    99n.9

Peirce, C. S., 80
Perl, Sondra, 6
Phelps, Louise Wetherbee, 8, 20

Reid, Joy, 43, 102n.18
Reither, James, 53
Richards, I. A., 19–20, 38, 77, 81,
    97n.3, 98n.5, 99n.7, 104n.26,
    107
Ricoeur, Paul, 11, 98n.5
Rodgers, Paul, 16, 17, 28, 33, 34,
    46, 48, 53, 95, 98–99n.6, 108

Rumelhart, David, 98 n.3
Russell, Bertrand, 31, 45, 48, 88–89, 91

Scardamalia, Marlene, 5
Selinker, Larry, 99 n.6, 107
Shaughnessy, Mina, ix, 1, 2–3, 11, 14, 16, 66, 68, 104 n.23
Shor, Ira, 16, 104 nn.22, 23
Sloan, Gary, 11, 31, 33, 38–39
Sommers, Nancy, 5
Stein, Gertrude, 99 n.7
Stein, Nancy, 98 n.3
Stotsky, Sandra, 32, 98 n.4, 105 n.27
Strunk, William, 29

Tate, Gary, xiv, 111
Trimble, Louis, 99 n.6, 107

van Dijk, Teun A., 18, 34, 97 n.2
Vygotsky, Lev, 25, 80–81, 105 n.27, 107

Watson, Wendy, xiii
Watzlawick, Paul, 100 n.11
Wayne, Don, xiii
White, E. B., 29
Widdowson, H. G., 107
Wilden, Anthony, xiii, 100 n.11
Winograd, T., 107
Winterowd, W. Ross, 13, 39, 98 n.4, 100 n.14, 111
Witte, Stephen, xiii, 9, 86–87, 98 n.4, 105 n.28
Wu Jing-rong, 45, 88

Xu Yong-hui, 45, 47

Zhu Wei-fang, xiii, 45–47, 69–71

Richard M. Coe received his Ph.D. in 1972 from the University of California, San Diego. He is currently Associate Professor of English at Simon Fraser University, Burnaby, British Columbia. He is the author of many articles, including the prize-winning "Rhetoric 2001," and a previous book, *Form and Substance: An Advanced Rhetoric*. He has taught in Canada, China, and the United States.